THE INNER JOURNEY TO CONSCIOUS LEADERSHIP

Ten Practices for Leading Consciously

PAUL WARD

BALBOA.
PRESS

A DIVISION OF HAY HOUSE

Balboa Press books may be ordered through booksellers or by contacting:

Balboa Press
A Division of Hay House
1663 Liberty Drive
Bloomington, IN 47403
www.balboapress.com
1 (877) 407-4847

Print information available on the last page.

ISBN: 978-1-5043-9983-8 (sc)
ISBN: 978-1-5043-9985-2 (hc)
ISBN: 978-1-5043-9984-5 (e)

Library of Congress Control Number: 2018902947

Balboa Press rev. date: 04/30/2018

PRAISE FOR
THE INNER JOURNEY TO CONSCIOUS LEADERSHIP

Fascinating, thought-provoking, and insightful! This book is a wake-up call to all those who think they are conscious of how they affect others. A must read for those who know they need to be better.

—Richard Leider, bestselling author, *The Power of Purpose,*
Repacking Your Bags, and Life Reimagined

Through his ten practices in *The Inner Journey to Conscious Leadership*, Paul Ward offers a wonderful overview of the skills, characteristics, and presence that leaders need in today's rapidly changing and complex world. He shares parts of his own journey as well as clear examples, supportive quotes, and helpful references to many other thought leaders' work as further resources for learning and development. Thank you, Paul Ward, for bringing clarity and definition to this new paradigm of leadership."

—Alan Seale, Director of the Center for Transformational Presence;
author, *Transformational Presence: How to Make a Difference in a Rapidly Changing World and Create a World That Works*

Developing conscious leadership is a noble quest in today's world. Paul Ward has provided a rich resource for those who are pursuing this path. Filled with stories from his own experience and references to an outstanding range of resources, the book organizes a wide range of material into nine themes that fulfill the book's intention to "inspire, educate, and encourage." I highly recommend this book to current and aspiring leaders who want to bring their best selves into their work.

—Dr. Linda Hoopes, President, Resilience Alliance; author, *Prosilience:*
Building your Resilience for a Turbulent World

Paul Ward has masterfully identified practices that are essential for anyone aspiring to be a conscious leader. Becoming a conscious leader is a journey, and regular practices are critical if one is to continuously grow in self-knowledge and self-awareness. A great addition to the field.

—John Renesch, futurist, author, *The Great Growing Up*

This is a serious book for those who already know about conscious leadership but who aspire to a deeper level of exploration … those with more than a casual curiosity about awakened executive guidance. The scope of what is covered is expansive yet provides enough information and references to related resources, as well his own personal perspectives, to ensure there are no "light touches" on the topics addressed. Paul brings in plenty of first-person viewpoints and past experiences, but it never feels like the book shifts to being all about him. Each personal anecdote serves as an elaboration mechanism for an issue he is highlighting or a point he is making. Finally, he provides both conceptual frameworks for the topics covered and practical how-to instructions for operationalizing the practices.

—Daryl Conner, chairman, Conner Partners, Conner Advisory, and
Conner Academy

In this book, Paul Ward provides the reader with all the equipment necessary to undertake their inner journey to becoming a conscious leader. Like all experienced guides, he has provided context, a map, and a list of suggested supplies. And, he has woven in his personal experiences and reference materials to ensure it is a memorable and life changing journey.

—Thomas Eddington, CEO FutureShapers

The Inner Journey to Conscious Leadership is a well-researched book that provides valuable insight into the development of a conscious leadership team. I would recommend my entire leadership team read and discuss the avenues teams may take to enhance their journey toward developing conscious leadership. Acting in a positive way engendered by conscious leaders, results in tangible outcomes that transforms an organization.

—James Wissler, Retired Health Care Executive

This book is a must read for anyone wanting to become a more conscious, values-driven leader. I have known Paul Ward in his roles as student, teacher, and researcher of values-driven leadership for nearly twenty years and recommend reading this book. The practices and behaviors he has presented will act as an excellent guide for aspiring conscious leaders who want to make a more meaningful contribution to the world.

—Richard Barrett, Founder of the Barrett Values Centre, and Director
of the Academy for the Advancement of Human Values

An essential guide for leaders challenged to align boards, leadership teams, and key stakeholders to a more thoughtful business practice through greater awareness, service, and courageous action. Dr. Ward is a leading thinker who shares years of experience as a centered, high-impact leadership and organizational transformation coach and consultant.

—Andrew Cox, president, Strategex Business Solutions Inc. and New Mexico Business Excellence

The Inner Journey to Conscious Leadership is an important contribution to and expansion of the business management literature. While words like integrity, listening, committing, and learning are common to this genre, awareness and consciousness are less so. By focusing on the inner processes of leadership, and the mindfulness, inner reflection, and awareness of the leader—and then connecting these inner processes and awareness with relationship and responsible action—Paul Ward brilliantly captures the entire gestalt of inspiring people and strategically managing resources successfully. Thus, he leads the charge toward a greatly expanded way of thinking about leadership, one that we will hear much more about as the science and art of conscious business continues to evolve.

—Ron Nelson, Executive Communications Consultant

This book is a must read for any leader looking to evolve the culture of their organization. It's not only instructional on what to practice to become more conscious as a leader, it can also be used as a measuring tool to really test if you are walking your talk. Thanks to Paul for this valuable contribution to the field of conscious leadership.

—Rebecca Watson, Leadership and Cultural Evolution Coach; author, *Conscious Leadership and the Power of Energetic Fields*

We live in uncertain and challenging times. People are becoming more demanding. They expect a better quality of work. They want a better quality of personal life. Decisions we all make affect others around us like never before. We are all stakeholders in our own future. Whether it be in a traditional and established business, a non-profit entity, a small start-up, in the business of government, or in our personal lives, we all need a purpose. We look for clarity of vision to know where we are going and what success will look like. Paul's book offers a simple guide to identifying that vision and how to best to develop strategies and actions to achieve our goals. If you don't know where you are going, any road will get you there. Paul provides the tools, not only to help determine the destination, but how to get there.

—Anthony Williams, Coaching and Consulting Client

The Inner Journey to Conscious Leadership provides a detailed roadmap and concrete practices for becoming a conscious leader. But even if readers are not interested in conscious leadership, anyone using the Paul Ward's principles in their life will certainly see a positive transformation in their professional performance, their workplace, and even their personal relationships. I have found this book thoroughly researched and delivered in an easy-to-apply style.

—Peter Matthies, Founder, Conscious Business Institute

CONTENTS

ACKNOWLEDGMENTS

Writing this book has been a journey of discovery. I have drawn on personal and professional experiences of life and work in different countries, industries, organizations, and families. My reflections on those experiences have caused me to pause and take stock, to begin letting go of some of the past experiences, and to practice being in the present moment, yet all the while keeping an eye on the desired future state. I am grateful to the many teachers who have touched my life and whose teachings have found their way in some way or another into this book.

I am indebted to my esteemed colleagues at the strategy execution consulting firm Conner Partners for the wisdom, knowledge, and experience gained during my time spent there as intent architect serving clients experiencing transformational change. I am especially grateful to Daryl Conner for his inspiration and feedback and for his permission to include references to specific philosophies, tools, and techniques developed and used by the Conner Partners team.

I am grateful to Dr. Mariana Bozesan, an integral investor, cofounder of AQAL Capital and AQAL Foundation, and doctoral researcher, for her permission to quote findings from her research study, "The Making of a Consciousness Leader in Business."

I met Andrew Faas, author of *From Bully to Bull's-Eye*, while writing this book. I am grateful to Andrew for his insights and for his permission to include Vera's story of workplace bullying in this book.

Many thanks to Alan Seale, Daryl Conner, John Renesch, Anthony Williams, and Jim Wissler, who provided valuable feedback on early drafts of the manuscript. Your insightful feedback gave me the confidence to continue the writing journey and refine the conscious leadership practices and behaviors initially presented. A special thank you to Janice Summers for your masterful editing of the final manuscript, and to Richard Bonk and Cosmic Webb for the cover design.

I am an avid reader and have included many references to the works of other authors who I have learned to value and respect. Although there are many references, maybe too many, my learning from these sources has provided a foundation for my thinking, and the metaphor of the dwarf standing on the shoulders of giants is the feeling I have as this book becomes a reality.

I am grateful to the many friends and family members who have been a source of inspiration and encouragement during my writing journey. I look forward with eager anticipation to the next book project combining the photographic skills of my brother Rob Ward with my own emerging writing talents.

And finally, thank you to all of you who read this book and embrace the ten practices for leading consciously. I hope you will enjoy your never-ending inner journey to conscious leadership and help make the world a better place to live and work.

FOREWORD

When it comes to Conscious Leadership, Paul Ward is an astronomer and a biologist—he looks through both a telescope and a microscope. His book gives the reader a big picture overview of the subject as well as practical, specific details on how to live and lead consciously. His big ideas of *Noticing What is Going On, Setting Intention,* and *Acting Responsibly* form the basis of a radical new way of leading in the world. Had he only introduced us to those concepts, he would have done the world of leadership an excellent service, but he gives us so much more. His detailed practical next steps form a roadmap with every necessary waypoint for the beginner and the more advanced practitioner of conscious leadership.

I smiled when I first saw on Paul's website that he is a hot-air balloon pilot. As he pursues his passion for ballooning, he takes people higher and higher on an adventurous ride. He does the same in this book. I found myself more engaged with each chapter, paying deeper attention to each new insight into conscious leadership. Unlike the balloons he pilots there is no hot air in this book. In fact, in a relatively short book, Paul manages to bring to bear the work and insights of countless contributors to the field of consciousness and leadership. This man has done his homework and practiced what he advocates in Chapter 2, *Learning Relentlessly.* He is a relentless learner.

Paul is not only a theorist and thinker about conscious leadership, but also a practitioner—he eats his own cooking. His stories about his journey and process give three-dimensionality to what could be flat if it were left at the conceptual level. I particularly valued his description of his own pilgrimages in Africa and the boundary waters of Minnesota. He has been a disciple, devotee, and docent, describing all the treasured artifacts along the consciousness journey. It's also easy to read a book like this and wonder if the author is a genuine, authentic, and approachable person. Paul's willingness to be vulnerable, to reveal himself and his shadows authentically give his voice even more credibility.

I appreciate that Paul moves beyond conscious leadership as an individual sport and speaks to the power and priority of the collective. His section on Organizational Leadership is a compelling, clarion call for all of us to apply consciousness to the whole. His distinctions between conscious capitalism and conscious business will answer many of the questions people have been asking about capitalism and whether it can be truly conscious.

Decades ago when Paul and I began our work in the world, the category of conscious leadership didn't exist. In recent years the concepts of mindfulness, presence, awareness, responsibility, and sustainability have become more commonplace. Regularly, I'm asked by leaders and organizations to bring conscious leadership as a program. They don't want just leadership training or team building or change management, creativity or innovation. They want training in conscious leadership. Even though this is increasingly the case, the collective conversation has not fully clarified a definition of conscious leadership. I believe Paul's book contributes significantly to this discussion.

I've spent my adult life supporting leaders who want to be the most exquisite version of themselves they can be. For me this process is all about waking up, seeing myself and others and the world more clearly. My work is about having transformational conversations with leaders. I have many of these discussions every week and from my perspective, Paul Ward and *The Inner Journey to Conscious Leadership* will make all the interactions about leadership more profound, more productive, and more applicable.

In the book, Paul says, "My intentions as author and teacher were to show up in the book as inspirational, educational, instructive, thought-provoking, practical, serious, and engaging." To that, I say, well done my friend. You have succeeded, and all the readers of this work and I are the better for it.

—Jim Dethmer, Co-founder, The Conscious Leadership Group

INTRODUCTION

Conscious leadership has been discussed for more than thirty years, and numerous books have been written, with no consensus on a single definition. Even the word *leadership* lacks a consistent definition, although it may be simply described as an interactive process in which leaders engage followers to achieve intended results. John Renesch, a thought leader in the field of conscious leadership since the mid-1980s and a personal inspiration behind the writing of this book, defines conscious leadership as a state of mind that includes heightened awareness of what is needed for the whole and taking responsible action based upon that awareness.[1] In other words, awareness with responsible action. The purpose of this book is not to provide a new definition of conscious leadership but, instead, a framework of practices to support those aspiring to become more conscious leaders.

A FRAMEWORK FOR CONSCIOUS LEADERSHIP

Adding intention to awareness and responsible action provided the three high-level themes of this book—noticing what is going on, setting intention, and acting responsibly. Three practices have been included for each theme. Listening with all the senses, learning relentlessly, and living mindfully are the three practices for noticing what is going on. Exploring purposefully, thinking possibility, and committing to action are the three practices for setting intention. Speaking candidly, acting with integrity, and taking responsible action are the three practices for acting responsibly. Each of these practices may be considered separately, but combining all the practices, and practicing all the practices all the time, represents the tenth practice.

It might be worth explaining how the term *practice* is being used in this book. Most of us have experience of practice from our childhood where, for example, we may have practiced playing a musical instrument.

In our home growing up, we had a pedal organ, sometimes referred to as a pump organ or harmonium, requiring constant pedaling to pump air to generate the sound when the keys were pressed. This was eventually replaced with an electronic organ and then with a more modern keyboard. While I was stumbling over the notes as I learned to read music, my mother would always say, "Practice makes perfect," and we all know that the answer to the age-old question, "How do you get to Carnegie Hall?" is "Practice, practice, practice." The term *practice* is both a noun and a verb, spelled the same in American English but different in British English, where the verb is spelled practise. Practice is defined in the *Oxford English Dictionary* as the customary, habitual, or expected procedure or way of doing something; and the repeated exercise in, or performance of, an activity or skill so as to acquire or maintain proficiency in it. Practices, as defined by Andrew Pickering, author of the *Mangle of Practice*, refer to specific sequences of activities that, if occurring repeatedly, may become a way of being and doing.[2] The practices described in this book are ways of leading consciously that, if practiced, will support your journey toward proficiency in conscious leadership. Behaviors are the specific things we say or do. For each of the practices that provide the framework for this book, specific conscious leadership behaviors have been described. Of course, repeating specific behaviors or sequences of behaviors can lead to new or different practices.

The practices in this book align well with an emerging movement in leadership studies known as *leadership-as-practice* that views leadership as occurring as a practice rather than residing in the attributes or traits of individuals.[3] This movement is concerned with how leadership emerges and unfolds through day-to-day experience rather than the dyadic relationship between leaders and followers. Leadership-as-practice is less about what one person thinks or does and more about what people may accomplish together. A perceived advantage of leadership-as-practice is that practitioners adopting this approach are better able to understand and reflect on their own actions and, consequently, better able to reconstruct their activity in light of their reflections and on behalf of their mutual interests. The leadership style approach reflects patterns of leadership behaviors. The idea of a recurring pattern of behavior is similar to leadership-as-practice, particularly when combined with situational leadership theory and practice. Rather than focusing on patterns of individual behavior, leadership-as-practice emphasizes the patterns of connected actions. Whereas the leadership styles approach focuses on the leader's behavior and is therefore leader centered with an emphasis on the practitioner, the relational leadership approach focuses on activities taking place within interactions and relationships with others. Although the practices described in this book are individually focused, the goal of becoming a more conscious leader is less about leadership personalities, traits, or competencies and more about serving others and the greater good, much of which requires a collective, collaborative approach. Many of the conscious leadership behaviors, activities, and practices described in this book may be found in the collective nature of leadership-as-practice and reflect people who lead and collaborate from a place of trust, not fear.

Conscious leadership is a journey, not a destination. Malcolm Gladwell, in his book *Outliers*, contended that "you need to have practiced, to have apprenticed, for 10,000 hours before you get good" but also recognized that practice alone is not a sufficient condition for success.[4] Many factors affect our degree of success. Unlike a top athlete whose goal is to be the best in their chosen sport, the conscious leader is not focused on winning, not trying to be the best *in* the world but to be the best *for* the world. It is an unending journey of becoming a more conscious leader. Although the practices presented in this book are quite simple, they are not easy. It will take dedication, a leap of faith, and daily practice to journey toward conscious leadership.

Imagine an iceberg, with behaviors and results visible above the waterline. Below the waterline and mostly invisible are mindsets, thoughts, feelings, emotions, and values along with our underlying physiology. We can make changes in our visible behaviors quite easily; however, sustaining these behaviors over the long term requires practice and more significant changes in the factors below the waterline. For each of the practices in this book, behaviors of aspiring conscious leaders have been described and summarized at the end of each chapter. The lists of behaviors are not exhaustive but illustrate the types of behaviors exhibited by conscious leaders.

MY JOURNEY TO CONSCIOUS LEADERSHIP

Why have I been called to write this book about conscious leadership? Although I have always been curious about leadership, I can trace my conscious leadership journey back to a meeting with Richard Barrett in New Jersey in 2000. Barrett, an author, speaker, and now an internationally recognized thought leader on the evolution of human values in business and society, was inspirational, and I immediately signed up for his values-based Cultural Transformation Tools certification program held in the Smoky Mountains of North Carolina. I applied these Cultural Transformation Tools based on the seven levels of consciousness[5] in coaching and consulting assignments and in the research for my doctoral dissertation. In my doctoral research study, I explored the influence of leadership values, behaviors, and styles on employee engagement.[6] This deep dive into leadership behaviors continued as a member of the faculty in a school of advanced studies, facilitating leadership classes and serving as a dissertation chair and committee member with doctoral students.

A management consulting career, initially with PA Consulting Group in the United Kingdom, then Quest Worldwide in Europe and the Americas, and Conner Partners in the United States, provided opportunities to work with organizational leaders across a broad spectrum of industries, where I served as an expert advisor on performance improvement and strategy execution projects. I am grateful to Steve Smith, founder of Quest Worldwide, who regrettably passed away while I was writing this book, and Daryl Conner, founder of Conner Partners, both of whom have been wonderful mentors in my consulting journey. I'm also grateful for the colleagues and clients who have enriched my journey to conscious leadership. This project and team leadership experience has been complemented by leadership and management roles at PA Consulting Group and General Electric Industrial Automation. I have also served as chair of the board of directors for a not-for-profit organization and president of the board of trustees for a liberal religious congregation.

Recent inspiration has come from John Renesch and Tom Eddington, cofounders of the FutureShapers organization. The mission of FutureShapers is to inspire, support, develop, and accelerate the consciousness of leaders in executive positions so that their organizations become more functional, effective, conscious, socially responsible, and life affirming.[7] Conversations with members of the FutureShapers community and beyond provided wonderful insights into the broad range of perspectives on conscious leadership.

In writing this book, I have taken a generally positive look at practices for leading consciously and provided specific behaviors that will support a leader's journey to becoming a conscious leader. Only occasionally have I used contrasting or negative behaviors that illustrate characteristics of unconscious leaders. I have drawn on my extensive coaching and consulting experience, my academic studies, my life experiences, and the writings of experts in this emerging field of conscious leadership and conscious business. Names of the people in the stories have been changed, and client organizations referred to have been described in a way that avoids identification. I like to think of myself as an alchemist, taking valuable ingredients from different places and applying them in my world. Sources of information have been cited throughout the book and references included in a section at the end, along with a list of resources I have found most valuable in considering what to include in this book and what to leave out. My hope is that, with this book, I am supporting and contributing to the expansion of conscious leadership in the world.

BEYOND CONSCIOUS LEADERSHIP TO CONSCIOUS BUSINESS

Although this book describes practices for becoming a conscious leader in any walk of life, people most likely to read this book are organizational leaders. Having spent much of my working life helping leaders and organizations through significant transformations, this book would not be complete without a chapter on how aspiring conscious leaders contribute to the businesses they lead. Conscious leadership is one of the four pillars of the conscious capitalism movement. Conscious businesses in the for-profit and not-for-profit world cannot exist without conscious leaders. The conscious business chapter provides a brief introduction to how conscious leaders are creating conscious organizations.

HOW TO READ THIS BOOK

This introduction provides an outline of the contents of this book. The sequence of the chapters has been selected consciously to provide a sense of flow from awareness and living mindfully to purpose, intention, and commitment, and finally to acting responsibly. Reading the book in the sequence presented may help deepen the understanding of the conscious leadership framework and each of the practices. The framework provides a series of containers, and although you can read chapter by chapter, selecting specific chapters will enable a deep dive into any of the individual practices. If you are looking for a high-level summary, read the final chapter first. As you read, think always about how the ideas expressed in this book apply to you and your role as you journey toward becoming a more conscious leader. Continually ask three questions:

- What are you noticing?
- What are your intentions about what you are noticing?
- What responsible actions will you take in response to what you are noticing?

WHY READ THIS BOOK

So many books have been written about leadership, and an increasing number of books about conscious leadership. So, why read this book on conscious leadership? My intention in writing the Inner Journey to Conscious Leadership was to inspire, educate, and encourage the application of practices and behaviors for leading consciously. Using a simple framework of conscious leadership practices, I have provided valuable insights into the emerging field of conscious leadership, practical tools for leading consciously, and shared experiences and stories to illustrate the real-life application of the practices. Noticing what is going on around you, setting clear intentions, and acting responsibly will help you become a more conscious leader and build more conscious organizations.

This book is for leaders, and we are all leaders. Even if you don't consider yourself a leader, the practices in this book can be applied to simply living consciously as well as to leading consciously. The books, articles, and doctoral dissertations I have reviewed during the research for this book have provided a wonderful learning experience. Where a reference piques your interest, I invite you to look more deeply into the source. Understanding, applying, and practicing the tools and techniques described in this book will help you shape your future, live more consciously, and make progress along the journey to becoming a more conscious leader.

I hope this book will be seen as supporting the expansion of conscious leadership in the world. I want to make the world a better place to live and work. Conscious leaders have a responsibility to serve as planetary stewards, making a meaningful contribution to the future of the world, their organizations, and the people whose lives are entrusted to them. I hope this book will help you shape your future with mindful awareness, purposeful intentions, and responsible actions.

PART I

Noticing What Is Going On

Listening with All the Senses

Conscious leaders are waking up and becoming more aware of themselves, of others, and of their environment. They are listening generously with all their senses, feeling all their feelings, and creating space for becoming more mindful and for noticing what is going on around them. This chapter is an invitation to begin waking up. Whoever you are—rich or poor, young or old, leader or follower—I invite you to accept this invitation to wake up, recognizing that conscious leadership requires us all to become wide awake and to stay awake and alert in all aspects of our lives.

A Zen Buddhist story reminds us about the importance of waking up and noticing what is going on. You may have heard the story before in one of its many variations. A man being chased by a vicious tiger comes to the edge of a cliff. As the tiger closes in on him, the man notices a vine leading over the cliff and down the precipice. Quickly he crawls over the edge and begins to climb down the vine, only to discover another tiger waiting for him below. Looking up, he sees a mouse gnawing away at the vine, his lifeline, and looking down, he sees the tiger. Just then, he spots a luscious strawberry within arm's reach. He seizes the berry and eats it. Ah, how delicious the strawberry tastes. Can you stop and notice the beauty in your environment and the people around you despite all the tigers and the mice?

In this chapter, we will explore how conscious leaders listen generously using all their senses, feel all the feelings, increase their self-awareness, become more aware of others and the environment around them, and create space for mindfulness.

LISTENING GENEROUSLY

Active listening has been part of leadership skills training curriculums for many years. Leaders have been encouraged to talk less and listen more, to make eye contact, to lean in, to keep arms and hands open and relaxed, to avoid interrupting, to smile, and to encourage the speaker to continue with a nod of the head or a short verbal comment. Listening generously requires much more than active listening. As Thomas Merton, a Trappist monk and well-known Catholic writer, says, we must slow down to a human tempo so that we can begin to have time to listen.[8] This requires a level of stillness and silence to really hear what is being said, a concentration within ourselves and on the person speaking.

Our concentration is affected by barriers or filters that get in the way of our listening. Distractions are everywhere, whether conversations close by, pictures and noise from televisions broadcasting constantly, or our own inability to ignore our mobile devices. We may be feeling tired, hungry, or stressed out. The speaker may be telling a long, boring story that we have heard many times before. We may be looking forward to something coming up later in the day. We may be, consciously or unconsciously, applying listening filters; we may be dismissing what the person is saying as insignificant, trying to diagnose the problem and thinking of ways to fix it, or becoming defensive. Managing these barriers and letting go of these filters can help with our concentration.

Silence and stillness are prerequisites for listening generously. Listening is not just waiting to speak. It's about listening to others without interruption, without simultaneously preparing what you want to say next. I see this in my young grandchildren. I often speak with them via Skype video conference. They are full of energy, dancing around the room and sitting down in front of the camera for just a few seconds at a time. They want to share the excitement of their day, and I am happy to listen. I don't need to be preparing to speak; I'm happy to share in their excitement. Stillness comes only at the end of the day, at story time, when they are listening to their favorite bedtime stories, which I love to read when visiting. Silence and stillness while listening to a client, colleague, or friend are just as important. The silence provides the space for them to speak; the stillness inside us provides the space for us to listen. Allowing the space for silence takes practice. Following Mahatma Gandhi's guidance "to speak only to improve on the silence" is wise advice for the conscious leader.

Rachel Naomi Remen, one of the pioneers in the mind/body holistic health movement, said, "When you listen generously to people, they can hear the truth in themselves, often for the first time, and in the silence of listening you can know yourself in everyone." Watching someone really listen generously to another without interrupting has been a personal privilege during my leadership training classes. The speaker often reports the positive emotions experienced when being listened to so intently, sometimes sharing something deep and meaningful for the very first time.

"The ear of the leader must ring with the voices of the people" was how Woodrow Wilson put it. More than that, listening generously is an important practice for conscious leaders, and I am reminded of Winnie the Pooh, who suggested, "If the person you are talking to doesn't appear to be listening, be patient. It may simply be that he has a small piece of fluff in his ear." Becoming a conscious leader requires us to make sure our ears are free of fluff. But listening with our ears is not enough. We need to be listening with all our senses.

FEELING ALL THE FEELINGS

How often, when listening, have you noticed the feelings in your body? We are familiar with the physiological changes, such as the butterflies in our bellies and the sweat on the palms of our hands when feeling fearful, the tingling sensation down the spine when feeling joyful, tightness across the shoulders and the back of the neck when feeling angry, and the welling up of tears in the eyes when feeling sad. Locating these feelings in our bodies and understanding the sensations is critical to listening with all the senses. This brings us to the feelings and emotions required to really notice what is going on in ourselves and others.

Feelings and *emotions* are words often used interchangeably, but although closely related, they are two distinct terms. Antonio D'Amasio, professor of neuroscience at the University of California and author of several books on these topics, explains feelings this way: Feelings are mental experiences of body states that arise as the brain interprets emotions, themselves physical states arising from the body's response to external stimuli. As an example, the order of events could be "I am threatened, experience fear, and feel horror."⁹ An emotion can be considered a physical response to change that is hardwired and universal. Feelings can be described as mental associations and reactions to emotions that are personal and acquired through experience. I have found Dr. Alan Watkins's integrated performance model, referred to in the introduction to this book, to be helpful in distinguishing between feelings and emotions.¹⁰ Watkins, an international expert on leadership and human performance, represents the integrated performance model as an iceberg. At the bottom of the iceberg, submerged below the waterline, is our physiology, where the primitive fight-or-flight response may be found. The next layer up in the iceberg is emotions. These emotions, sometimes described as e-motions or energy in motion, can be both positive and negative and drive our feelings. These feelings determine our thinking. Our physiology, emotions, feelings, and thoughts—all internal and invisible—drive our external and visible behaviors and the results we achieve at the tip of the iceberg.

Conscious leaders exhibit high emotional intelligence. Building on Harvard University professor Howard Gardner's theory of multiple intelligences described in the book *Frames of Mind*,¹¹ Daniel Goleman introduced the now-familiar and well-researched concept of emotional intelligence in his 1995 book *Emotional Intelligence: Why It Can Matter More Than IQ*, which was followed by *Working with Emotional Intelligence* in 1998.¹², ¹³ Goleman, an internationally known psychologist and best-selling author, describes emotional intelligence as the capacity for recognizing our own feelings and those of others, for motivating ourselves, and for managing emotions well in ourselves and in our relationships.

In the book *Primal Leadership, Realizing the Power of Emotional Intelligence*, Goleman and his coauthors described the four dimensions of emotional intelligence: self-awareness, self-management, social awareness, and relationship management, all competencies and skills that can be learned and that align well with the practices of conscious leadership. Also described is a continuum of leadership styles that was a critical input to my own doctoral research study into leadership values and behaviors.¹⁴, ¹⁵ The continuum of styles runs from commanding and pacesetting through democratic, affiliative, coaching, and visionary. The last four of these leadership styles foster resonance, whereas the first two can readily generate dissonance when not used effectively. Goleman et al. described an interesting research study of 3,871 executives. The results showed that, all other things being equal, leaders who use a style with a positive emotional impact saw decidedly better financial returns than those who did not, and leaders with the best results didn't practice just one particular style but many of the six distinct styles, depending on the business situation.

The Complete Coherence Universe of Emotions app has been designed to help develop emotional intelligence.[16] Mapping two thousand emotions out of an estimated thirty-four thousand emotions found so far and represented as a planet or a star shows active and relaxed emotions on a vertical axis and positive and negative emotions on the horizontal axis. This is an excellent tool for building our vocabulary of feelings and emotions and increasing emotional literacy. As we learn to name the emotions and how we feel about the emotions, we can increase our ability to feel all the feelings and recognize how these emotions and feelings influence our thoughts, which in turn influence our behaviors. We can begin to take control of our emotions, mastering what is going on below the surface while knowing that our feelings are within our control and it is not someone else who is doing it to us.

The death of a loved one or birth of a child often accentuates feelings and emotions. We may vividly remember where we were when we heard news that affected us deeply. When my mother passed away in England in 2014, I was working on a client site on the thirty-eighth floor of the General Motors Building in New York City. I received an email from a family member asking me to call my father as soon as possible. Although my mother had not been ill, and I had seen her only a few weeks before, I knew this was not good news. I stepped outside the office building and called my father. He had my number but in his heightened emotional state was unable to remember how to add the international code. My mother had passed away that morning. An abdominal aortic aneurism had ruptured the day before, and her death had followed quite quickly.

I remember walking across Fifth Avenue and into Central Park to gather my thoughts and call my brother in California, as my father had asked me to do, and then to call my wife in Florida and my children in England. The immense sadness over the death of my mother was immediately limited by the need for responsible action. I was scheduled to facilitate an all-day workshop the following day. In these situations, clients are understanding, but this was a workshop I didn't want to miss. And anyway, I didn't have my passport with me and would have to return home to Florida before flying to England. The tension between my own grief and my responsibilities to my father and to my client brought forth a cacophony of feelings. I felt intense sadness at my mother's unexpected passing. I felt a little angry about the timing. I felt overwhelmed by the need to make immediate decisions. Fortunately, my brother was working at home and was able to begin the journey to England within hours of our telephone conversation. He would be with my father the following day. My daughter in England was already taking care of his immediate needs. I was able to facilitate the workshop and follow my brother across the Atlantic two days later. I felt the roller coaster of emotions during the workshop, alternatively feeling absorbed in facilitating the process, sad about my mother's passing, and yet thankful for a family vacation only a few weeks earlier where four generations of our family had lived together in a converted barn for an entire week.

Increasing our sensitivity and awareness of our emotions and feelings will help us notice what is going on inside of us and in others. When we feel changes in our bodies, such as goose bumps on the back of the neck or butterflies in the stomach, we know something is happening and we had better sit up and take notice. We can check in to assess why we feel that way and begin shifting our negative feelings to a more positive place. Rhythmic breathing has been shown to help shift away from negative emotional states such as anxiety, anger, and frustration toward positive emotional states such as passion, determination, and focus. Naming the emotions and feelings for ourselves and, where appropriate, for the person we are in dialogue with can help us notice what is going on.

AWARENESS OF SELF

Self-awareness is the first component of emotional intelligence, and having a deep understanding of our emotions may be considered a minimum foundation for becoming a conscious leader. In addition to emotions, self-awareness also means understanding our strengths, weaknesses, needs, and desires. Conscious leaders cultivate deep self-awareness.

Building self-awareness requires us to penetrate the commotion and distraction of our lives. Matthew Crawford, a philosopher and motorcycle mechanic, writing about becoming an individual in the age of distraction, noted that attention has become an acute collective problem of modern life. We are becoming used to intrusive advertising everywhere—on our computer screens, on the free apps on our mobile devices, in the airport, at the gas station, and more. Crawford describes bus riders in Seoul, South Korea having coffee smells spritzed into the air and up their noses that complement the advertisement playing over the bus's sound system just before it stops outside a well-known coffee chain.[17] Our distractibility in these public places is, to a great extent, understandable, but to what extent are we distracted in our private thoughts and conversations?

We are often distracted by our thoughts, feelings, and emotions. Rather than seeing the negative quality of the distraction and trying to avoid being distracted, can we reframe the distraction as a messenger? Rather than getting so absorbed in the distraction that we miss the content, can we be present in the midst of the distraction, discovering how to navigate and learn from the distractions in daily life rather than trying to eliminate the them? We will explore being present in more depth in the chapter on living mindfully.

Reducing or reframing our distractibility and increasing our attentiveness requires greater self-awareness. I am reminded of the often-quoted phrase, "We do not see things as they are, we see things as we are." So, how can we increase our self-awareness along with our ability to increase our attentiveness? Getting to know ourselves better is an important first step.

The Johari Awareness Model, often known by the more familiar name the Johari Window, originally developed by California professors Joseph Luft and Harry Ingham in 1955, remains an interesting self-awareness tool for understanding relationships with ourselves and others. Joseph Luft's book, *Of Human Interaction*, has been in my library for many years and provides a valuable explanation of the Johari Window.[18, 19] Imagine a window with four panes of glass whose sizes can be changed by moving the intersecting vertical and horizontal dividers. The four panes of glass or quadrants of the window represent awareness of behavior, feelings, and motivation and signify what is known to ourselves and others based on a self-assessment. The top left quadrant is the open or arena quadrant, representing what is known both to self and to others. The top right quadrant is the blind spot quadrant, representing what is not known to self but known to others. The bottom left quadrant is the hidden or façade quadrant, representing what is known to self but not to others. The final quadrant, bottom right, is the unknown quadrant, representing what is not known to self or to others. Assessment scores, when plotted on the window, result in quadrants or windowpanes of different sizes. For example, limited self-awareness may show up as narrow left-hand windowpanes and, where others can see our behaviors, could represent a large blind spot caused by low self-awareness. Conversely, we may keep hidden from others certain aspects within our self-awareness. Self-disclosure can increase the size of the hidden windowpane, demonstrating to others greater self-awareness.

The shape and size of each quadrant may change depending on the situation and the interaction, particularly in the bottom left hidden or façade quadrant where we have a choice about self-disclosure. Early in a relationship, I typically limit the extent of self-disclosure, sometimes being reluctant to share my private feelings and reactions or what I am noticing about what is going on. In my coaching or consulting roles, I initially seek to encourage clients to share more about themselves than I do as an advisor, yet greater personal self-disclosure can encourage greater reciprocal interaction and disclosure on the part of my clients. Similar disclosure issues arise in the early stages of a love affair. Self-disclosure may be used to increase levels of attractiveness, but there are risks to both over-disclosure and under-disclosure. In both client and personal relationships, disclosing too much can create as many problems as disclosing too little. Strict control over self-disclosure can create distance in a relationship, whereas lax control over self-disclosure can result in relationships becoming too close too quickly. Greater self-awareness enables us to consciously choose the degree of self-disclosure appropriate for the situation.

What we don't know can hurt us. This is true for aspiring conscious leaders as well. With this in mind, we must be careful to avoid confusing self-awareness with self-delusion. Shelley Reciniello suggested that this idea of self-delusion, this lack of self-awareness, is the single biggest trap for a leader, and in order to avoid these fantasies and delusions, leaders must be open to self-knowledge and how they are actually perceived by others.[20] Kevin Cashman, CEO at Korn Ferry and author of *Leadership from the Inside Out*, cited a survey of business executives where they were asked, "Are you in the top 10 percent of leadership performance?" Ninety percent said yes! The accuracy of self-assessment is clearly questionable, and Cashman recommends using inside-out self-assessments along with outside-in observer assessments.[21] Observer assessments can be truly revealing to a leader with limited self-awareness.

This book is about practices for leading consciously, and as we are beginning to see, this takes concentration and hard work. Sometimes it is just easier to avoid being conscious. The motives for consciousness avoidance or a flight from self-awareness may simply be fatigue or laziness but may also be a fear of learning something we do not want to know. Nathaniel Branden, widely recognized as an expert on self-esteem, explores fear and pain as a motive for avoidance of consciousness, reminding us that contemplating thoughts or memories that stimulate suffering or anguish has no intrinsic merit, and the impulse to withdraw consciousness is not abnormal.[22] But pain is not a valid reason to go unconscious when we know actions need to be taken. We have all made mistakes that have had unfortunate consequences; contemplating our part in these mistakes can be painful. For example, sending an inaccurate or emotional reply-all email response can have us reaching for the recall option only to find the message has already reached the inbox of colleagues and even superiors. Although painful, reflecting on our actions and their consequences to understand the cause of our mistake, noticing what is going on inside of us, can help us become more mindful next time around and avoid repeating mistakes in the future.

Being aware of our intuitive abilities allows us to consciously access our inner knowing, understand something immediately, and make decisions based on instinctive feelings rather than conscious reasoning. We may consider intuition as a hunch, a gut feeling, or a feeling of knowingness. We all have intuition although often prefer to use our rational intellectual faculties to explore and understand a situation and come to a logical conclusion. The opportunity with increasing self-awareness is to tap into our intuition and develop a healthy balance of our intuitive and rational abilities. Rather than ignoring our ever-present intuitive feelings, developing greater awareness of how intuition influences our decisions can help us trust our judgment. How many times have you been in a group conversation where you find yourself not aligned with the majority view and concerned about an impending decision? The logical mind can see others' perspectives, but your intuition is screaming, "Going down this path will be a disaster!" Do you go along with the majority view to avoid appearing as the naysayer, or are you prepared to be vulnerable, sharing your intuitive feeling even when you don't have facts to support your position? Greater self-awareness can generate the confidence to give voice to your intuitive sense of what is right and what is wrong.

Our values and beliefs, including what we really stand for, are also an important part of our self-awareness. Values assessments have been conducted for many years and were a feature of my own doctoral dissertation. I have always appreciated Richard Barrett's seven levels of consciousness model used as a basis for personal and organizational values assessment.[23] I still have the results of my own Leadership Values Assessment. Perhaps most noteworthy was the 70 percent alignment between the set of values selected by my fourteen observers and the values I selected, indicating a high degree of self-awareness. Values drive our behaviors, and values awareness provides us with an understanding of why we do what we do and say what we say.

In our world that is increasingly social, interdependent, and transparent, feminine values such as empathy, inclusivity, cooperation, connectedness, humility, candor, patience, trustworthiness, openness, flexibility, courage, and vulnerability are ascendant.[24] These values are woven through *Shakti Leadership*, a book that embraces feminine and masculine powers in business. Authors Nilima Bhat and Raj Sisodia introduce Shakti, the divine mother, and remind us that conscious leaders are fundamentally selfless, distinguishing between false or ego-based power and true power.[25] True power is *power with* rather than *power over*, where no one has to lose for someone else to win. Understanding and living both feminine and masculine values are important for conscious leaders regardless of gender.

Beliefs are assumptions we hold to be true and arise from learned experiences, including cultural and environmental situations we have faced. Conscious awareness of our beliefs and how they are influenced by others and by our own situation can help us understand what is going on inside and how we make our decisions. Statements of belief have been featured for more than fifty years in the *This I Believe* series that originated on National Public Radio. These *This I Believe* essays, accessible on the website, in podcasts, and in books, provide a public dialogue about beliefs.[26] Writing an essay or simply writing a series of statements beginning with "I believe …" can help us increase our awareness of what we truly believe. In the spirit of self-disclosure, let me share some of my beliefs. I believe in the freedom of choice; in the inherent worth and dignity of every person; in peace, not war; in clarity of purpose and responsible action; in the power of dreams and the power of positive thinking; and that there are always multiple right answers in every situation. Pause for a moment and write down or bring to mind five "I believe …" statements.

Listening with all our senses increases our awareness. These sensations are revealed in our bodies and in our thoughts. Conscious leadership author Rebecca Watson suggests that for raising our levels of consciousness, we can simply write down the thoughts that are causing the state of consciousness we find ourselves in. We can then decide to explore different thoughts that will lead to a more desirable state of consciousness, from which we can take actions that will lead to a different outcome.[27] With advancing technology, using electronic devices for recording our thoughts also works well. Continuously practicing self-awareness can help us wake up and become more conscious leaders. Our self-awareness can also be developed through a daily mindfulness or contemplative self-reflection practice and by seeking feedback. Living mindfully will be explored in a later chapter.

AWARENESS OF OTHERS

Greater awareness of ourselves is required before we can truly improve the awareness of those around us. Once we are truly noticing what is going on inside of us, we can shift our attention to others. Noticing what is going on in ourselves and others is the foundation for conscious relationships.

A few years ago, I stayed at the YMCA of the Rockies Estes Park Center as part of the Sounds True Wake Up Festival. Arriving early, I took the opportunity to explore some of the hiking trails surrounding the park. The trails were quiet, and the walk in the woods provided an opportunity for reflection and solitude after the long flight and drive to the center. After a while, I saw through the trees a magnificent male elk. I stepped carefully through the trees and managed to take a couple of photographs of this splendid animal. The photographs were fine except for the fallen tree that covered part of the elk's legs. I couldn't get a better picture and carried on with my hike through the woods. Returning a little while later, I saw the elk lying down in a small clearing and decided to try to get closer for a better picture. After a while, he stood up, wary of my presence. I felt a real connection to this mighty elk standing tall and motionless looking warily back at me. I took a couple of photographs, but this bull elk had had enough of my intrusion. I learned afterward that elk are among the noisiest of ungulates. Barking, bugling, squealing, and chirping are all sounds attributed to this member of the deer family, but the loud grunt accompanied by a shake of the head with those huge antlers was a clear signal to me that I was too close. The huge animal was not aware of my feelings of awe and wonder, but I was soon aware that my relationship with this elk was at an end. This experience with this magnificent elk has stayed with me and serves as a frequent reminder of the importance of my awareness of others, of all sentient beings.

Noticing what is going on in others and in our relationships with others is important for the conscious leader. Bringing consciousness to each encounter allows us to see, hear, feel, and sense what is going on and respond in a way that enables us to convey attentiveness and respect, and that allows the other person to feel heard and understood. In addition to our awareness of our own thoughts, feelings, and sensations, we must increase our awareness of the thoughts, feelings, and sensations of others. One of the common concerns expressed by people in organizations is, "My manager isn't listening to me. He or she is looking out of the window—or worse, at their computer screen or mobile phone." Conscious leaders remove these distractions. Having mastered our distractibility and the need to fix the problem being described by the other person, we can quiet our own mind and create the silence to listen attentively using all our senses. This is more than simply maintaining eye contact. This is about listening to the words being spoken, the tone of voice, the emotion in the voice, and the body language. It is also about hearing what is being hidden and not being said, and about listening attentively without judgment.

Silence in a conversation can sometimes feel uncomfortable, and we often feel the urge to interrupt the silence with our own voice. Conversations with one of my clients, the CEO of an international manufacturing organization, always included periods of silence. I would ask a question or make a statement, expecting an immediate response, but this business leader often took what felt like an unusually long time to think before responding. At first, I found myself filling the silence by adding to what I had said, but I soon learned to feel comfortable in the silence, confident that this leader would answer in his own time. My eventual awareness of this leader's need for silence and the value of silence in conversations made me a better coach.

The practice of noticing requires us to be comfortable with, and appreciative of, the silence, to be mindful of what is going on and to simply be with the other person. We have all experienced being with a friend or family member after the passing of a loved one. Words are not necessary; just being with that person, holding them with our hands and our heart, is sometimes the best we can do. Our awareness of the needs of the other person can help us control our desire to jump in and break the silence. In communication skills training, we are often invited to offer reflection and restatement of what the person said, and this can be a good practice to encourage the person to continue speaking, but if we are worrying about what we are going to say, we may not be using all our senses to hear the other person. Simply listening, being there in that moment, may be all that is necessary. Our silence can heighten our awareness of and sensitivity to the person we are with. We increase our self-awareness as we increase our awareness of others and our environment.

AWARENESS OF OUR ENVIRONMENT

The word *environment* often evokes images of the natural world and the sustainability of our planet, and this is important, but context determines the consciousness and awareness appropriate for our situation. Noticing what is going on in the larger environment is important but noticing what is going on in our immediate environment, where we are right now and where we may be in conversation with others, is essential for the conscious leader. We will come back to the larger environmental issues when we discuss the practice of acting responsibly, but to continue our focus on awareness of ourselves and others, we will concentrate on our immediate environment and the need for creating the space for mindful awareness.

CREATING SPACE FOR MINDFULNESS

As we have already noted, our world is full of distractions, and our distractibility is a challenge to our mindfulness and awareness. Janice Maturano, former VP at General Mills, founder of the Institute for Mindful Leadership, and author of *Finding the Space to Lead*, observed, "We often simply do not have the space, the breathing room, necessary to be clear and focused, and to listen deeply to ourselves and to others."[28] According to Jon Kabat-Zinn, creator of the original mindfulness-based stress-reduction program, "Mindfulness means paying attention in a particular way: on purpose, in the present moment, non-judgmentally."[29] This is a simple concept whose power lies in practice and application. Mindfulness creates the space for awareness. The conscious leader practices mindfulness with intention and responsible action.

Creating space for mindfulness is related to our physical, mental, emotional, and spiritual needs. Creating the right physical environment for our own contemplative practices allows us to quiet the mind and become aware of our thoughts and emotions. For our interactions with others, creating the right physical environment is also important. When we plan conversations in small groups or maybe with just one other person, removing distractions and barriers to the free flow of information helps us be more attentive to others and ourselves. In larger groups, the location and setup of the room is important. Where possible, I like to sit in circles with low or no tables in the center. Creating the best physical space allows us to give full attention to what we are doing and to be aware of our own thoughts and emotions and notice what is going on with the other people in the circle. This awareness enables a concentration that can make us more awake, attentive, and able to listen.

Our thoughts about what we're going to say can also limit the space for awareness about what the other person is saying. Delaying thoughts about what we want to contribute to the conversation can leave more capacity to listen with all our senses to what is going on in the room. Controlling our ego and desire for self-gratification from speaking our mind may leave space for greater awareness of the visible and sometimes invisible goings-on in others in the room. In the classic psychology experiment, children were given the option of having one marshmallow immediately or, if they were able to wait fifteen minutes, to have two marshmallows. Some were unable to wait and ate the marshmallow with little or no delay, but about a third of the children succeeded in delaying immediate gratification and were rewarded with the two marshmallows.[30] The reward for postponing thoughts about what we want to say may not be in the opportunity to speak, but in noticing much more than we might have otherwise, had the mental space not been occupied by formulating our response.

Our emotions also take up space. We can see this in the media and political talk shows where someone is so incensed about a particular issue they do not listen to what the other person is saying and become increasingly emotional and often less coherent. Noticing our emotions resulting from statements by others can help us become aware of our own feelings about the comments and about the person. Simply noticing the changes in our emotional state can help us manage those emotions and leave space for increasing our awareness of what is going on in others. When it comes time for us to speak, we can then come from a place of awareness and control and offer our contribution to the conversation in a calm and coherent manner.

A practice of breathing, noticing, and feeling the sensations in our bodies can help create space for mindful awareness of what is going on in ourselves, in others, and in our environment. This does not mean we avoid conveying what we believe to be true. Holding the space and taking a stand are not mutually exclusive.

NOTICING WHAT IS GOING ON—LISTENING WITH ALL THE SENSES

Conscious Leadership Behaviors:

- Waking up, becoming increasingly aware of everything
- Listening attentively using all the senses
- Feeling all the feelings
- Developing emotional intelligence
- Being highly sensitive to emotional and physiological changes in ourselves and others
- Appreciating the silence
- Being aware of feminine and masculine values within ourselves and others
- Trusting intuitive feelings
- Managing the environment to limit distractibility; embracing distractions as messages
- Creating the space for becoming mindful of what is going on

CHAPTER 2

Learning Relentlessly

Conscious leaders are constantly curious—curious about themselves, curious about others, and curious about their environment. When working with leaders, I look for curiosity. If they are not curious, they are unlikely to want to change. Learning relentlessly is about remaining open to new ideas and insights; checking understanding rather than making assumptions; creating space for learning both individually and in groups; accepting mistakes and failures as learning opportunities; giving and receiving timely, constructive feedback; and constantly growing in self-awareness.

RELENTLESS LEARNING

Young children are inherently curious, constantly asking questions. They come from a place of simply not knowing. It is fun to watch them with a new toy and observe the joy of discovery as they find new ways to play. They are comfortable with not knowing. As we get older, we appear to get increasingly uncomfortable with not knowing. During my thirty years as a management consultant, I have been privileged to work in many organizations, industries, and countries around the world. Each new client seemed to be in a very different industry than the one before, and the first day on-site, while I was keen to impress people about my expertise, I often knew very little about the organization or their industry. Being able to arrive and be comfortable in a state of not knowing allowed me to be curious and begin a new learning experience, often requiring me to leave my ego at the door. This level of not knowing allows for a highly inquisitive and energetic curiosity, where we are not trying to fix a problem or prove a point. Rather, we are following one of Stephen Covey's seven habits of highly effective people—seeking to first understand before attempting to be understood.[31] If our egos take over, we'll stop being students of our craft, stop being curious, and start acting as if we know all the answers.

My last full-time consulting experience was at strategy execution consulting firm Conner Partners, where Daryl Conner and his leadership team created a wonderful learning culture. I attribute much of my recent personal growth to the time spent with the change leaders at Conner Partners and with our clients. At Conner Partners, we identified five ways we inhibit our own growth as practitioners:

- We restrict ourselves to only the tangible aspects of change and fail to listen with our hearts and intuition for messages and guidance
- When we listen, we fail to accurately understand the messages and guidance we receive
- When we understand, we fail to believe what we hear
- When we believe what we hear, we fail to follow the guidance provided
- When we heed the guidance, we fail to follow it consistently— doing the difficult things only when they are easy or convenient

To overcome these inhibitions, we must practice relentless learning.

When I was four or five years old, I had a large-wheeled tricycle, blue with white mud guards and a single caliper brake on the front wheel. Some of my friends had two-wheel bicycles with stabilizers or training wheels. The training wheels allowed them to ride their two-wheel bicycle without falling off. As they lost balance and leaned to the left, the left-side training wheel would keep them from falling off and allow them to find balance until the right-side training wheel came into play. I remember watching one of my friends the day the training wheels were removed, his dad running along beside him giving confidence and support where the training wheels used to be. The fear of falling gradually receded, and my friend gained the confidence required to ride without stabilizers, training wheels, or parental support. For some reason, when I progressed to a two-wheeled bicycle, painted green as I recall, my dad didn't provide stabilizers or training wheels. It was only a small bicycle, and on tiptoes, I could reach the ground on both sides. I soon found my confidence and my balance, and despite a few accidents over the years, I remember fondly both my blue tricycle and my first green bicycle and the ultimate progression through various stages of pedal-power bicycles to eventually owning a motorcycle. Numerous major and minor accidents were all part of the continuous learning experience. I have always had good balance, although not always confidence in my ability to avoid accidents. I have always had to rely on a natural curiosity and a desire for learning relentlessly, learning from others as well as my own mistakes.

We can all recall times in our lives where we experienced dramatic growth when we learned something significant about ourselves or about life—an "aha!" moment. These moments often occurred during challenging times or periods of adversity. Often there was a teacher, a guide, a mentor, a coach—someone to balance the bicycle without the security of the training wheels. Craig Neal, coauthor of *The Art of Convening*,[32] has been one of my valued mentors. Long before he coauthored the book, Craig invited me to join him on a men's wilderness journey, an expedition in the Boundary Waters Wilderness Area within the Superior National Forest in northeastern Minnesota, close to the Canadian border. Eight men, with heavy sixty-pound backpacks and large nineteen-foot-long canoes, leaving all electronic devices behind, embarked on a six-day journey into the wilderness. There were many learning experiences during these six days, one of which remains a vivid memory for me.

For this journey into the wilderness, I trained for ten weeks to be well prepared for portages and ready to carry a sixty-pound backpack and a two-man canoe. I had taken the training very seriously, hiking parts of the Appalachian Trail close to my home in New York to build the strength and confidence needed. Despite this physical training, during the journey I encountered an insurmountable obstacle while on a long portage over and down a high ridge. I had volunteered to carry one of canoes, which weighed forty-two pounds, as well as my backpack, which weighed at least sixty pounds. I set off with the weight of both the backpack and the canoe on my shoulders. Initially, I found the going tough, but I was making good progress. It was all about the balance I had learned on my bicycle. Then I came to a large rock formation across the path. It wasn't that high, but it was high enough to make stepping over it a difficult task. With the canoe and the backpack weighing me down, I could not get my foot to the top of the mound, and the damp, sloping sides made it difficult to climb. I made a few attempts, but it soon became clear to me that, without help, this was an insurmountable obstacle. Someone lifted the canoe off my shoulders, allowing me to climb over the rock, but the damage was done. I was already feeling exhausted. I couldn't complete the portage carrying both of these heavy loads, but with the help of others, I made it to the next lake. I learned a valuable lesson that day—I am not strong enough to complete my journey through life without the help of others, many of whom are recalled in this book. My appreciation for their help is immense.

GIVING AND RECEIVING FEEDBACK

Working with Daryl Conner in his change execution consulting practice was a relentless learning experience for me. In his *Change Thinking* blog series about learning as a foundation for our work, Conner reminds us that mistakes are inevitable and even essential to the learning process. He describes a learning sequence reflecting clear patterns displayed by people who view missing the mark as a corrective experience rather than a failure. Corrective experiences occur when mistakes lead to learning and growth. Here, the person recognizes that a performance gap has taken place, acknowledges the negative implications and takes responsibility, apologizes to those affected for any adverse repercussions, identifies causes and the appropriate healing or mitigating actions to pursue, applies the proper remedy to reduce the likelihood of recurrence, and shares learnings so that others may benefit from his or her experience. Failures occur when mistakes lead to stagnation and atrophy. Here, the person is unaware or uninterested when a performance gap occurs, deflects the negative implications and his or her responsibilities, ignores those affected, evades exploration of causes and actions to be taken, sidesteps application of remedies so recurrence of the problem is likely, and withholds from others any key learnings that occur. People who view missing the mark as a corrective learning experience receive constructive feedback comfortably, listen with an open mind, and learn from the experience.[33]

As part of our process of learning relentlessly, we all need to receive feedback, and we often have valuable feedback to offer others. Yet, giving and receiving effective feedback is not easy. The gift of feedback, both reinforcing messages of genuine appreciation and constructive comments focused on improvement, is often delayed, postponed, or overlooked completely, thereby missing important learning opportunities. We all like to receive recognition and appreciation for the things we do. In part, this is to satisfy our egos, but it is also about learning from the experience. Some of us are very self-critical. If I fail to receive feedback, I may resort to imaginings, the introspective voices than can be so damaging to self-esteem and consequently to performance. Reflecting on my performance, I imagine what others might be saying. The voice inside my head focuses on failures: it was not one of my best performances, it was a long way from peak performance, it was a struggle. Then I might say, "I can't do this" or "I am not as good as them." Constructive feedback from others helps me know what to keep and what to change, builds confidence, and enables personal growth.

We often anticipate that the experience of receiving feedback will be negative and uncomfortable, raising doubts and fears rather than building confidence and capability. For me, I recall that, when I announced my intention to embark on a bachelor's degree program, my father's reaction was to introduce doubt, not only about my four-year commitment but also in my ability, which, I agree, had not been well demonstrated to that point in my educational journey. Despite his ultimate support and his enthusiastic attendance at multiple graduation ceremonies, his negative feedback lodged in my memory for more than thirty years. Maybe the doubts he expressed increased my resolve to succeed, but I suspect, had he expressed belief rather than doubt, suggestions rather than misgivings, my confidence would have been higher, and I would have appreciated his feedback more, and invited it more often. I will say more about my father's reaction in Chapter 5: *Thinking Possibility.*

We need to be open to feedback, comfortable enough to ask for guidance and to engage in conversation with the person giving the feedback to ensure understanding and consider potential changes as a result of the learning. If your initial impulse is to reject, ignore, or disagree with the feedback being given, ask for more information about what was said, paraphrase and reflect back to check understanding, and share your perspective without negating the legitimacy of the other person's viewpoint. If your initial impulse is to agree with the feedback, state what aspects of the feedback seem accurate and why and then discuss the learning and possible corrective actions. Regardless of whether you agree or disagree with the feedback, express appreciation for the contribution. Receiving feedback can be uncomfortable in the moment, and it is important to take time for quiet reflection, to notice what was going on, and to learn from the feedback received.

Giving constructive feedback requires self-awareness and the awareness of others and the contextual environment discussed in the previous chapter. Offering feedback in person as soon after the event as possible is desirable, but it is important to take time to prepare the feedback and look for uninterrupted private time for the conversation. In giving feedback, stay focused on your own observations and possible implications, and avoid sounding judgmental. Toastmasters International, a worldwide membership organization with a purpose of helping members improve their communication, public speaking, and leadership skills, recommends the sandwich technique—beginning with a positive, acknowledging the merits or positives about the person or the situation, followed by the meat of the constructive feedback, and ending with another positive, reinforcing observation. This can work when offering feedback on a presentation at a Toastmasters meeting, but when using this sandwich technique, the meat of the feedback can get lost in the thick slices of positive reinforcement. Speaking candidly, another conscious leadership practice explored later in this book, requires us to be frank and straightforward, to be specific about our concerns, focusing on behaviors or actions, giving specific examples and suggestions for improvements, and sharing the consequences for addressing and not addressing the feedback offered. Having offered feedback, it is important to check for understanding and agreement, and offer time for additional conversations to support the learning from the situation.

As conscious leaders, we still need to earn the right to influence others. Not everyone is open to feedback and willing to listen. Offering uninvited feedback may not help a relationship. I like to say, "I have some feedback that I would like to share with you. Would you be willing to listen to what I have to say?" Even then, the person may not accept the feedback. At Conner Partners, we practiced *passionate neutrality*. We might advocate strongly and passionately with our feedback but be committed to remain neutral and unattached to the outcome. We have a responsibility to offer feedback, and the receiver has the choice about whether to accept and act on it. Practicing passionate neutrality—being unattached to the outcome—enables the aspiring conscious leader to offer feedback without being judgmental.

Giving feedback may seem easy at times but giving effective feedback can be challenging. Skills and techniques for giving effective feedback are essential, and timing is important. However, this is all about the doing. For me, giving and receiving effective feedback is about both doing and being, which we will explore further in the next chapter. When receiving feedback, I need to be open to the messages, prepared to make changes if necessary, and grateful that another has prepared such valuable gifts. When giving feedback, I need to be compassionate yet at the same time courageous, considerate yet direct, nonjudgmental yet straightforward. Giving and receiving effective feedback is truly a gift for both the receiver and the giver—a gift we can keep on giving.

PARADOX OF POLARITY AND DUALITY

When more than one thing is held to be true at the same time, we call that a paradox. For leaders, these often show up as dilemmas where we feel forced to make a choice. The idea that paradoxes must be reconciled is, according to John Renesch, a myth requiring unnatural and inaccurate labels often resulting in the creation of a false truth for the sake of maintaining this intolerance.[34] The concept of passionate neutrality introduced in the last section is an example where we can advocate strongly yet remain neutral and accepting of the outcome. This brings to mind F. Scott Fitzgerald's observation that the test of a first-rate intelligence is the ability to hold two opposed ideas in mind at the same time and still retain the ability to function.[35]

Exploration of the paradox of polarity and duality is not new. First published in 1908, the fourth Hermetic principle, the principle of polarity stated, "Everything is dual; everything has poles; everything has its pair of opposites; like and unlike are the same; opposites are identical in nature, but different in degree; extremes meet; all truths are but half-truths; all paradoxes may be reconciled."[36] Although many teachers suggest polarities must be managed, for conscious leaders, awareness and acceptance of polarities is an important starting point.

The practices and behaviors described in this book may at times appear to be contradictory. Sometimes this is a matter of timing, but often, holding apparently opposing, potentially contradictory perspectives or behaviors can provide a valuable balancing of these paradoxes. This balancing of opposites can be thought of as managing polarities. Rather than thinking of polarities as contradictions, they may be viewed as interdependent entities that do not function as well when considered in isolation from one another. Managing polarities enables what may look like irreconcilable differences to be perceived as reciprocal elements of the same whole. Choosing one approach without due consideration of the other may only serve to create new problems. Successful breathing requires both inhaling and exhaling; it is not possible to achieve the intended outcome of continuing to live without both aspects of breathing.

Other examples of interdependent polarities you may encounter while reading this book include:

- Being nonjudgmental while still having the courage to challenge inappropriate behaviors
- Living in the moment while holding a vision of the desired future state
- Setting a clear intention while retaining flexibility to change direction as needed
- Encouraging individual autonomy while seeking team cohesion
- Inspiring collective responsibility while taking personal responsibility
- Promoting participatory leadership while having to make seemingly autocratic decisions

It is easy to get caught up in the allure of a particularly attractive polarity. We only have to look at today's political landscape to see the effect of polarization: it is easy to be attracted by one perspective only to find out that it is not at all what it at first appeared. The story of the Abilene Paradox provides an excellent example of how easy it is to go along with a group's apparent agreement of a single perspective when no one truly believes the proposed direction is the best approach.[37] The story is set in Texas on a stifling hot July afternoon in a home without air-conditioning but with a fan, cold lemonade, and a game of dominoes that required very little exertion. All was well until the father suggested a trip to Abilene some fifty-three miles away to have dinner at the cafeteria. The unspoken reaction of one family member was, why embark on a fifty-three-mile journey in hundred-degree heat in a non-air-conditioned 1958 Buick? But all too quickly, not wanting to sound negative, one by one, each family member expressed their support for the idea, and they set off. The heat was brutal, the dust joined with perspiration and became caked on their skin, and the cafeteria food was unappetizing to say the least. Returning home after the long four-hour car journey, recriminations began, with each family member blaming the others for wanting to go to Abilene when, as it turned out, no one really wanted to go. Each had done just the opposite of what they really wanted, which was to stay home. Had they considered the upside and downside of each of the options, staying at home potentially bored but relatively comfortable compared with a four-hour uncomfortable car journey to a mediocre cafeteria, this family may never have made the trip to Abilene. How often have you reluctantly gone along with the apparent majority only to find out later you had the majority opinion if only you had given voice to it?

Polarity thinker and founder of Polarity Partnerships, Barry Johnson, introduced polarity mapping using a grid that plots the upside and downside of two apparently contradictory poles bringing the whole picture into focus, which helps us visualize both-and thinking.[38] The map has four quadrants, with each axis or pole having an upside and a downside. Upsides are about the positive results obtained when we focus on that pole, and downsides are about the negative outcomes present when we overfocus on this side without paying attention to the other side. Alternatively described as the polarity two-step, neuroscientist and leadership coach Alan Watkins suggests that recognizing the upside and downside of apparently polarizing perspectives enables us to be alert to the warning signs in order to rebalance before dropping into the downside of either polarity.[39] Finding the best of both worlds rather than choosing one or the other enables more effective polarity management. Learning about managing polarities and how to hold apparently opposing, potentially contradictory perspectives, actions, or behaviors is an important starting point.

Reaching higher levels of consciousness through increased awareness may enable us to move beyond duality—the positive and negative, the good and the bad, the conscious and the unconscious—and realize that, rather than separating the opposites, a focus on unifying and harmonizing opposites may help with discovering a place that transcends and encompasses the opposites. This concept of non-duality has been described as the philosophical, spiritual, and scientific understanding of non-separation and fundamental oneness.[40] Detailed analysis of non-duality is beyond the scope of this book but an increased focus on oneness rather than separateness is worthy of more detailed exploration on the journey to conscious leadership. Cultivating the ability to embrace and live with non-duality and paradoxes based on increased awareness is the inner work of the conscious leader.

The meditation experience may be considered a paradox. On the one hand, it is about completely letting go of everything, and on the other hand, it is about paying more attention. It is about letting go of everything and having the courage and conviction to keep letting go, fearlessly, no matter what arises, yet without letting go of attention, without letting go of awareness, and continually noticing what is going on around us. It means having both a deep acceptance of *what is* through the letting go and at the same time having a profound yearning for something else based on what we are noticing. Conscious leaders can work and live in these two places simultaneously.

LEARNING YOUR TRIGGERS

We all experience triggers in our lives, something that happens that creates a reaction. According to emotional intelligence pioneer Daniel Goleman, the amygdala in the emotional center of the brain sees and hears everything that occurs to us instantaneously and is the trigger point for the fight-or-flight response.[41] As we have already seen in the previous chapter, increasing our sensitivity and awareness of our emotions and feelings helps us notice what is going on inside ourselves and in others. Learning about these emotional triggers and how we react to the triggers is essential for becoming a more conscious leader.

Positive emotions can be triggered when we see something of beauty or when someone appreciates us. When one of our children or grandchildren performs at an exceptionally high level or wins a special award, this experience may trigger excitement, even joy. These are good feelings to have, but more often, we think of triggers as our negative reactions to what people say or do. I enjoy watching all kinds of sports, and baseball in particular provides many examples of players and managers being triggered by the decisions of the umpires. The water cooler in the dugout has been attacked by numerous players angry at an umpire's decision, including Yankee right fielder Paul O'Neill, whose meltdowns were nearly as memorable as his home runs and exceptional catches in right field. Dugout violence against inanimate objects has almost become a Major League Baseball tradition, but these behaviors are not acceptable in our normal working environments.

We can all think of people in our lives who trigger us or push our buttons, and although we may not go as far as destroying a water cooler, the emotional reactions that cause a negative change in behavior diminish our performance and our relationships with those around us. Knowing who or what triggers our negative emotions is the first step in learning from these emotional triggers. Words can trigger these negative emotions. Emails, instant messages, and texts have replaced many in-person conversations. The brevity of the written communication and the inability to hear the tone of voice can cause significant, often unintended, reactions, and the desire to respond immediately with an angry reply-all message can be overwhelming. Stephen Covey provided an excellent description of Viktor Frankl's experience in the death camps of Nazi Germany, where he was able to decide within himself how what he observed and experienced was going to affect him: Between stimulus and response, there is a space. In that space is our power to choose our response. In our response lies our growth and our freedom.[42] When I receive an email from someone who triggers me or when I read an email that stimulates an emotional reaction, I flag the email for later reply, creating the space between the stimulus and my response that allows a more conscious and thoughtful answer.

Emotional triggers are often a result of fear, frustration, humiliation, embarrassment, stress, and even physical discomfort, sometimes caused by illness, hunger, fatigue, or medication. These triggers are also caused by our beliefs, based on what has happened to us in the past. Unresolved anger is a significant cause of workplace tensions, conflicts, and disagreements that result in poor individual and team performance and lower productivity. Taking an inventory of your anger, your triggers, your hot buttons, and who and what causes your frustrations should not be postponed. Noticing these triggers and consciously choosing our responses to them is an important part of our relentless learning.

Think about someone or something that recently triggered a negative emotional reaction in you. You may have suppressed your emotions or, conversely, displayed an emotional reaction that you later regretted. Whatever our reactions in these situations, we may view them as learning opportunities—triggers that show up for our awakening and growth. In *Shakti Leadership*, Nilima Blat and Raj Sisodia suggest that the conscious leader is flexible, and in cultivating flexibility when triggered or challenged, we should ask the following questions:

- What do I need to learn from this experience?
- What about this person's behavior triggers me? In what way am I perhaps also like that?
- Is that something I need to acknowledge rather than deny? Better still, is there something in this denied quality that may be something I need?
- How does that relate to who I am? What part of me is being reflected in this situation?
- What do I need to claim about myself that would make me a little more whole?[43]

Reflecting on the triggers in this way enables us to increase our self-awareness, from which we can develop responses that contribute positively to our own performance and the performance of those around us. Rather than covering up or camouflaging our emotional reactions, we may be able to learn from the experience and share our feelings, revealing more about ourselves in a constructive way and building better relationships with others. Sometimes we are not even aware of being triggered, and therefore miss the opportunity to take a time-out, even just for a few seconds, to check in and ask, "How am I really feeling right now? What is my current state of being?" These questions can help bring our attention to our current state of consciousness.

Much of this work on understanding and learning from people and things that trigger our negative emotions is inner work, part of our inner journey. We have discussed incidents that trigger emotional reactions. Learning from these experiences is essential for the conscious leader. However, truly conscious leaders have typically experienced life-changing triggers that have caused significant personal transformations. Dr. Mariana Bozesan is an integral investor, cofounder of AQAL Capital and AQAL Foundation, and doctoral researcher. In her study of the *Making of a Consciousness Leader in Business,* Bozesan asked her sixteen doctoral research participants to share their most significant emotional, mental, physical, and spiritual experiences that triggered their own transformation.[44] Bozesan defines consciousness leaders as people who have evolved to postconventional levels of interior development and are engaged in globally sustainable wealth creation for the benefit of all. The research participants in her study were all consciousness leaders characterized by material abundance and outstanding external success in the business world. This characterization may be much narrower than the aspiring leaders reading this book, but the research findings reflect many of the practices explored here. Bozesan's masterful analysis and synthesis of her research findings are well worth further reading, and I invite you to obtain a copy of the manuscript. Here are a few of her findings that appear to align well with the practices for leading consciously that are presented in this book and that relate to the inner journeys of conscious leaders:

- Consciousness leaders appear to have developed to higher levels of consciousness through an evolutionary process that included peak experiences, significant transformational experiences, or exceptional human experiences.
- Based on the premise that pain is part of life but suffering is a choice, consciousness leaders were able to use emotional, physical, spiritual, or other kinds of pain as an agent for awakening and deeper transformation.

- Although material abundance and outstanding external success in the business world characterized all consciousness leaders in the study, all of them without exception seem to have arrived at the conclusion that more money and material gain will not enhance how they feel and relate to other human beings and their environment. As a result, they have transcended the importance of money and material gain in their lives.

- Living in the spotlight of public lives, consciousness leaders face the challenge of having to live up to the demands of external success at the expense of their interiorities. Therefore, facing their shadows has become a decisive component not only of their interior transformation but also of their ongoing consciousness leadership ability.

- Consciousness leaders indicated that fear has been a tremendous teacher. By confronting their greatest fears, they reached higher levels of consciousness and transformed in all areas of their lives, internally and externally.

- Eventually, all consciousness leaders arrived at a point in their lives when their interiority had to be reconciled with their exteriority. Not living in line with their interiorities was no longer tolerable, and they felt morally and ethically obliged to come out, speak up, and live with the consequences.

- Consciousness leaders confirmed that as they evolved to higher levels of understanding and consciousness, they were able to access a different kind of information and wisdom that is helping them achieve more with far less effort.

- The three phases of the consciousness leaders' journey, like Joseph Campbell's Hero's Journey, are (a) the Awakening of the Consciousness Leader, (b) the Initiation of the Consciousness Leader, and (c) the Emergence of the Consciousness Leader.

- All research participants confirmed without exception that their internal transformation took place over many decades and referred to a journey of trial and error that is an incredibly painful, slow, and messy process.

- All consciousness leaders in the study reached higher levels of emotional mastery, with gratitude, love, compassion, joy, and appreciation as their dominating emotions.

I am grateful to Dr. Mariana Bozesan for her permission to include these findings here.

The triggers that initiate significant turning points in our lives may include the death of a loved one, a divorce, a health condition, such as a potentially terminal disease or a recognition of becoming significantly overweight, the unexpected loss of a job or a traumatic career move, or simply a recognition that there must be more to life than what we are currently experiencing. These triggers often lead to extensive reading about personal transformations, and this can reveal potential teachers, which in turn encourage an exploration of meditative or spiritual practices and may involve physical journeys for self-exploration in other environments or cultures. These personal journeys create the internal space for emotional, mental, physical, and spiritual experiences that often lead to a life-changing transformation. Personal transformations often represent periods of relentless learning.

Although I look back on my strict religious upbringing, with its fear-based teachings and proclaimed exclusivity, and the loss of a baby brother and baby sister during my formative years as challenging, on reflection, I did not experience the acutely negative childhood experiences that many have faced. Protected from the evils of the outside world until I left home at nineteen, I found myself naïve and unprepared for the journey ahead. Despite this, I followed a quite traditional path of getting married and having children, furthering my academic education, and striving to make career moves that would enable me to provide for my family and continue the acquisition of material assets. Although I can point to numerous milestones and turning points along this journey, it wasn't until I took two transformative journeys outside of my comfort zone in my late fifties that I really began to appreciate the possibilities of personal transformation. The first experience was the men's wilderness journey referred to earlier in this chapter. The second was an inventure in East Africa led by Power of Purpose author and executive coach Richard Leider, where the adventure of a walking safari was combined with an inner journey of discovery.

My inventure in East Africa was a fifteen-day walking safari across the Serengeti, sleeping in tents erected by a support team, and unplugged from all electronic devices. Conversations around campfires and during long treks across the plains, personal reflections during quiet periods of solitude, and daily journaling provided opportunities to get back to the rhythm in the place where the original people on earth emerged. I set no specific goals and embraced this inventure as a learning opportunity: learning about the region, the animals, and the way of life of the people of the Hadza and Maasai tribes; learning about my fellow travelers and Richard Leider's power of purpose; and, perhaps most importantly, learning about me and my own life's journey. Here are three complete-the-sentence exercises about the time of my life I learned then and use today:

- It is too late in my life for me to …
- It is too soon in my life for me to …
- It is the right time in my life to …

The list of completed sentences for the last question were and remain today much longer than the list of completed sentences for the first two statements. Although I didn't experience any epiphanies or sudden realizations during the inventure, I can trace many of my subsequent directions back to the learnings from this experience. Purpose became a core feature of my coaching, and I began research into purposeful aging. This led to the acquisition of 2Young2Retire®, a business focused on supporting people through transitions into the second half of life, to an increasing focus on conscious leadership, and ultimately to the writing of this book. The inner transformations that began during that inventure continue today.

GROWING IN SELF-AWARENESS

Relentless learning offers the opportunity to notice what is going on inside and around us and enables us to continue growing in self-awareness. This increase in learning will bring a complementary growth in self-confidence. From a basic curiosity, through learning how to give and receive effective feedback, appreciating the paradox of polarity and duality, understanding what triggers us day to day and the triggers that influence our inner journey, this practice of relentless learning is an essential feature of our inner journey to conscious leadership.

NOTICING WHAT IS GOING ON—LEARNING RELENTLESSLY

Conscious Leadership Behaviors:

- Being constantly curious
- Encouraging learning through curiosity
- Seeking honest feedback
- Giving effective feedback
- Accepting mistakes as learning opportunities
- Asking what can be learned from an experience
- Creating space for learning individually and in groups
- Managing polarities as interdependent elements
- Understanding negative emotional triggers and responding thoughtfully
- Using internal and external journeys to develop higher levels of consciousness

CHAPTER 3

Living Mindfully

Mindfulness is a state of being aware of ourselves, other people, and our environment. We can remind ourselves to be mindful with a regular morning meditation practice or moments of mindfulness during the day or at the beginning of meetings, but conscious leaders aspire to live their whole lives mindfully. Living mindfully means being in the moment; it is about *being* as well as *doing*, about how we show up in the world, our character and presence, and leading from the inside out. It is about avoiding the drama triangle, practicing mindfulness, and living mindfully every day.

BEING IN THE MOMENT

Thich Nhat Hanh, a Buddhist monk, spiritual leader, poet, and peace activist, reminds us to be "washing the dishes to wash the dishes."[45] He notes two ways to wash the dishes: the first is to wash the dishes in order to have clean dishes, and the second is to wash the dishes in order to wash the dishes; while washing the dishes, one should only be washing the dishes, which means that while washing the dishes, one should be completely aware of the fact that one is washing the dishes and not thinking about the cup of tea we will be drinking after washing the dishes. Living in the moment is about being attentive to the present moment, living mindfully in that moment, without letting our thoughts drift into possible future situations. The past is already over, the future hasn't happened, we only have the now.

I was reminded of living in the moment, not replaying the past or anticipating the future, on the first night of my men's wilderness journey to the boundary waters, a region of wilderness straddling the Canada-United States border between Ontario and Minnesota. With no electricity, no telephone lines or cell towers, and no roads to the inner lakes, the boundary waters wilderness area is a place to get away from it all. We had driven the six hours from Minneapolis to the outfitters where we collected our gear and where we would put in to the lake to begin our canoeing adventure the following morning. Having erected the tents, eaten our first meal, and enjoyed conversations around the campfire, I found myself in a sleeping bag, sharing a tent with two other men. Sleep came slowly. I had not slept in a tent for more than thirty-five years, and I was embarking on a journey into the wilderness with seven other men I had never met before. *What was I thinking!*

The next day, we would leave for six days in the wilderness with no contact with the outside world and no easy way back to civilization. Did I really want to do this? I could go as planned or I could stay back, but whatever I did, I had to decide tonight. Panic and fear set in unlike anything else I can ever recall. I had to sit up inside the tent; I could not lie down. Climbing out of the tent was impossible without disturbing the others. I sat there shaking with fear about this impending journey. The question was, Should I go on this unknown journey into the wilderness or should I turn back now, before we begin? I don't know why this fear suddenly appeared. I had not been afraid at any time during the preparation, yet I experienced overwhelming fear in that moment.

After a while, the fear subsided. I had confidence in my guides, who had led these expeditions before, and in my companions, who were all on their own journeys through life. I knew I could go on this journey. I knew I could do it. I could overcome even this unexpected panic attack. I remembered the Zen Buddhist story of the monk, the tiger, and the strawberry. I knew that the wilderness would taste like that strawberry, and I knew someone would help take care of any tigers. The overwhelming fear of the unknown future was overcome, and looking back, this journey became one of the most transformative experiences of my life. Although we did a lot of hiking, paddling, cooking, cleaning up, and talking, I began developing an inner silence of being. I was to learn later that philosopher Lao Tzu had said many years ago, "The way to do is to be."

Living mindfully is about *being* rather than *doing*. Abraham Maslow, an American psychologist who was best known for creating Maslow's hierarchy of needs, identified fourteen values of being experienced by self-actualized people based on an analysis of their peak experiences: wholeness, perfection, completion, justice, aliveness, richness, simplicity, beauty, goodness, uniqueness, effortlessness, playfulness, honesty, and self-sufficiency.[46] This list of values or facets of being could also be attributed to the conscious leaders who practice being before doing.

"Being" mastery is one of Kevin Cashman's eight practices for mastery of leadership from the inside out.[47] This requires us to be mindful of our internal and external being. To stop doing and focus on being. After a mindfulness meditation at a recent workshop on leading consciously, one of the participants commented to me that it was the first time in as long as she could remember where she had not been doing something for that length of time. Cashman, in describing present-moment awareness, suggests that thinking about being in the present is not being in the present; it is thinking about being in the present. Simply being in the present moment requires letting go of the past and the future and increasing awareness by noticing what is going on around us. Tuning in to the present moment, despite the noise all around, allows us to be mindful of the present moment and focused on non-doing and non-thinking. This non-doing is about letting things be and allowing them to unfold in their own way.

Mastery of being requires us to accept the way we are and where we are on our journey. The capacity to have presence without resistance, to be present to everything that is happening in the present moment, creates possibility for the future. Present moments can be resonant, profound, and extraordinary but may also be challenging, uncomfortable, and tedious, and we may long for a mechanism that gives us the power to fast-forward through current uncertainties. Yet as keen as we are to touch the beautiful futures of our imaginings created during possibility thinking, we cannot get there if we are not fully present in the evolutionary experience of the now. If you are patient enough to stay in the present moment and take pleasure in your life unfolding as it will, the journey from one pinnacle to the next will seem to take no time at all. Quelling the urge to rush, to stay in the present moment, will enable you to witness yourself unfolding, learning, and becoming increasingly conscious. Know that, when the time is right, the passage of destiny cannot be blocked. Leading consciously is about knowing who we are, who we are being, and how we show up in the world.

CHARACTER AND PRESENCE

I am grateful to Daryl Conner for his deep insights into character and presence. The foundation for much of this section comes from his teaching and writing on this topic.[48] Simply stated, character is who we are, and presence is how we show up in the world. In other words, presence is a reflection of our character. Learning more about our character and presence will help us live mindfully.

Fred Keil, author of *Return on Character*, defines character as "our unique combination of internalized beliefs and moral habits that motivate and shape how that individual relates to others."[49] Character is who we are, our true nature, the substance of what we have to offer as human beings. American biologist, naturalist, and Pulitzer prize-winning author Edward Wilson offers a comprehensive definition of character in his book, *Consilience: The Unity of Knowledge*:

> True character arises from a deeper well than religion. It is the internalization of the moral principles of a society, augmented by those tenets personally chosen by the individual, strong enough to endure through trials of solitude and diversity. The principles are fitted together into what we call … the integrative self, wherein personal decisions feel good and true. Character is in turn the enduring source of virtue. It stands by itself and excites admiration in others. It is not obedience to authority, and while it is often consistent with and reinforced by religious belief, it is not piety.[50]

Our true nature is quite distinctive, and even with all the other commonalities we might share with others, we can still legitimately claim our individuality because of our unmistakable character. Our character is comprised of many features that may be considered either commendable or undesirable characteristics. The more commendable characteristics might include a passion for honesty and truthfulness, a commitment to service, or other values such as loyalty, integrity, or fairness, or more spiritual, philosophical dimensions. Undesirable characteristics might include being self-centered, manipulative, egocentric, narcissistic, or lacking empathy or compassion. Character is our true essence and changes slowly if at all, but being aware and mindful of our character, our true nature, allows us to control how we show up in the world.

If character represents who we are, presence is how this character is exhibited to others. We have all experienced a time of being in the presence of someone who is important and influential in our lives, or someone we look up to as a great leader. I recently had the privilege of meeting a Tibetan lama, the eighth Phakyab Rinpoche, founder and spiritual director of the Vision Healing Buddha Foundation and the narrator and coauthor of *Meditation Saved My Life.*[51] Rinpoche's story of growing up in the Himalayan mountains, imprisonment in China, arrival in New York with what turned out to be gangrene and tuberculosis, and his three years with the healing power of meditation in a small Brooklyn studio apartment is powerful enough, but to be with him was an incredible experience. His energy field was palpable. I knew I was in the presence of a very special human being and will treasure the memory in my mind as well as the photograph someone kindly took of the two of us together.

Presence is like a force field we project that represents aspects of our character. The presence leaders radiate can be described positively as powerful, constructive, empathetic, compassionate, loving, peaceful, or more negatively as self-centered, demanding, disruptive, or narcissistic. In any case, a strong presence represents a sphere of influence that may positively or negatively affect those who encounter this energy field. We may pay more attention to our physical appearance, our weight, hairstyle, and attire, than we do our presence even though this influence zone is likely to have a greater effect on those around us.

Although a leader's character is relatively stable, presence may vary considerably due to the environmental variables experienced on an ongoing basis. At the same time, because presence is a reflection of the leader's true nature, there will be a continuity to how it is projected. Although a leader's presence may vary due to the situation, the leader's true character will ultimately be revealed. Abraham Lincoln put it this way: "Character is like a tree and reputation like a shadow. The shadow is what we think of it; the tree is the real thing." Our presence, how we show up, is represented by the shadow we cast. Lance Secretan, one of the most insightful and provocative leadership teachers of our time, links character with service and says, "We serve each other, and the larger collective—earth, the universe, God— not through the doing that is described in so much of our goal-oriented management literature and teaching, but more through the being: who we are; not through our accomplishments, but through our presence; not from a social self, but through our essential self; not through our egos, but through our integrity; not through the force of our personality, but through the radiance of our soul. Character is who we choose to be— particularly when no one is looking."[52] If we are mindfully aware of how we show up, we may ask servant leader questions: How may I serve? How may I best serve the person I'm with? How may I best serve my organization? How may I best be of service to the world? Coming from this place of service enables us to be more attentive to how we wish to show up in the world as conscious leaders.

In linking character with reputation, Kevin Cashman contrasts the qualities of character and coping, observing that character transforms, opening up possibilities and multiplying energy, whereas coping reacts, dealing with circumstances and expending energy.[53] The transforming nature of character is guided by values such as authenticity, purpose, openness, trust, courage, and inclusion, whereas the reacting nature of coping is guided by image, control, fear, concern for self, and exclusion. Reputation reflects our character and how we show up in the world. We all know leaders who show up with all the answers, want to control the process and the outcome, and lead based on fear and ego. While short-term results are possible with this approach, sustainable change requires the transforming nature of our character and emphasizing service before self.

In a revealing study of return on character, respected leadership researcher, adviser, and author Fred Kiel identified four critically important behaviors or habits through which our character is expressed: integrity, forgiveness, responsibility, and compassion.[7] Two of the study's most critical findings were (1) there is an observable and consistent relationship between character-driven leaders and better business results; and (2) people demonstrate character through habitual behaviors, noting that people can develop the habits of strong character and unlearn the habits of poor character with better self-awareness. We will explore these habits and other behaviors later in this book when we explore the conscious leadership practices of acting responsibly.

We can develop our behaviors, how we show up, how we express our character, but Daryl Conner asserts that we can only nurture presence by evolving our character.[54] He says presence is a natural outcome of our character, a reflection of who we are, and trying to develop it directly usually generates more frustration than progress. Although we may consciously change our behaviors, we can't authentically alter our presence to reflect something inconsistent with our character, at least not for long. The presence we unfold in our relationships emulates our true nature, but it is not the fullness of who we are. If we want to nurture our presence, we must evolve our character. Character plus presence impacts how we are perceived. We might think of it this way: Character is like clay in the shape of our inner nature. Presence is a reflection of that shape in a mirror. Impact is the positive or negative experience people have when exposed to the mirror's representation. Strengthening presence by way of fostering character may appear to be an indirect path, but it is the only course possible. Trying to enhance an elusive reflection is pointless. If we want to have a more positive impact, we must work the clay instead of reaching for the mirror.

In *Love the Music You Play*, Conner suggests that playing the kind of music everyone expects may increase the number of listeners, but most of them will be spectators. Audiences receive much more benefit when they truly appreciate the music and the artist. If you see your task as increasing the size of the audience, it doesn't matter what music you play as long as it draws large crowds. If you view your role as that of a virtuoso for a specific sound, you should not only want to focus on playing that kind of music, you should primarily play for people who can appreciate it. The twist here is that, by limiting your audience, you gain instead of losing. You enlarge your true fan base by playing to a more select market. True fans are the ones who not only praise what you do but respect how you play.

My brother-in-law is a master musician. I first knew Bruce Molsky when he was a full-time mechanical engineer. Now he is one of the most revered ambassadors for America's old-time mountain music. A visiting scholar at the American Roots Music Program at Boston's Berklee College of Music, he still has time to travel the world playing and teaching his unique style of music. Many of his audiences are true fans with deep knowledge of him and his music. This doesn't mean that he avoids playing for audiences who show only a slight interest in his music. He knows it is important to be accessible to listeners who are unfamiliar with his work because, through exposure, they may become dedicated fans. Occasionally, I get to see him perform in venues such as the Lincoln Center in Manhattan or a small British pub on the outskirts of London, but sitting across from him in his upstate New York home or our Florida apartment allows me to witness his true character and his beautiful music in a more intimate setting. If I were to aspire to play the fiddle, banjo, or guitar, I can think of no better teacher.

As aspiring conscious leaders, we have our own unique musical style that blends what we do with who we are. Both are important. Bruce spends many hours honing his skills as a musician and refining every section of music he plays. His skills and talents are unquestionable, but he has a unique character and presence, without which he would not be held in such high esteem by his true followers. In his own words, "Performing and teaching traditional music is the biggest thing in my world. For me, being a musician isn't a standalone thing; it informs everything I do in my life. It's always been about being creative and being a part of something much bigger than myself, a link in the musical chain and part of the community of people who play it and love it."[55]

Daryl Conner says, "The finest music you'll ever play surfaces in front of appreciative audiences. To bring out your mindful best, your job is to:

- Know who you are and the leadership music that truly comes from your heart.
- Play that music with all the authenticity and passion you feel and broadcast your frequency as strongly as you can.
- Recognize that your ability to play the music as well as you do is a gift and strive to share it with people who resonate with its significance (others may be listening but play for your fans).

- Don't compromise your musical talent to gain a larger audience or to please certain listeners in powerful positions. Be who you are and build your leadership practices around that."

Living mindfully requires us to be fully aware of our character (who we are) and our presence (how our character is expressed) and, finally, the impact we are having on the world around us. Performing authentically, without reservation, to those who show up to listen will help us to be the best we can be. Remember, people won't care what you know until they know who you are and how much you care.

Extending the concepts of presence, Alan Seale describes transformational presence as "a state of being in which one lives, leads, works, and engages in life from a place of profound alignment with one's soul mission or life purpose, and the greater consciousness. This presence opens the door to the greater potential waiting to emerge at any moment, situation, or circumstance, and to becoming a steward for that potential to manifest."[56] The conscious leadership practices of exploring purposefully and taking responsible action align well with the interconnected nature of transformational presence. Closing the gap between awareness, mindfulness, and knowledge around the practices of noticing what is going on with the practices of setting intention and acting responsibly are explored in a chapter of Seale's book. Closing the gap between simple awareness and living mindfully requires attention to our character and presence.

LEADING FROM ABOVE THE LINE

No book about conscious leadership would be complete without reference to integral philosopher Ken Wilber's integral All Quadrants All Levels (AQAL) four-quadrant model and his recent focus on showing up, growing up, waking up, and cleaning up.[57] Showing up means taking all four quadrants of Wilber's AQAL model into account. Growing up relates to stages of human growth and development with awareness and mastery of each of our multiple intelligences. Waking up refers to the states of consciousness of waking, dreaming, sleeping, pure witnessing, and ultimately unity consciousness. Cleaning up includes both shadow work of fixing what is broken and the positive psychology of strengthening what is right, thereby enhancing our thriveability.

I am grateful to Alan Watkins for his simplified representation of the AQAL framework presented in an enlightened leadership model with the three dimensions of I (being, bottom left-hand quadrant); WE (relating, bottom right-hand quadrant); and IT (doing, top right and top left quadrants), where the being and relating are considered internal dimensions and the doing is considered an external dimension.[15] Although this book on conscious leadership is focused on practices and behaviors, the concept of being, relating, and doing maps to some extent on the three broad areas of noticing what is going on, setting intention, and acting responsibly. Watkins suggests that many business leaders are still convinced that driving results and business growth is basically all about goals, targets, and plans in the external dimension of doing, and the awareness of the potential of the other dimensions of being and relating is minimal. Much of Watkins's philosophy of 4D leadership is about balancing the internal and external dimensions. Although personally extremely goal driven for much of my life, my inner journey to conscious leadership has evolved with greater focus on being and relating. This balancing of being and relating with doing is an important feature of the practice of living mindfully.

Leading from above the line is another useful concept that helps us to be mindful about leading consciously. Jim Dethmer, Diana Chapman, and Kaley Warner Kemp, coauthors of *The 15 Commitments of Conscious Leadership,* describe four ways of leading, two ways below the line and two ways above the line.[58] These four ways of leading represent four states of being that people move into and out of constantly. Being mindful of the state we are in at any moment allows us to move between states and shift where appropriate from below the line to above the line. We can describe these four states as a progression, but it is important to note that we do not process through the states as if they were stages of development. We frequently shift between states unconsciously, but as we become more mindful of the state we are in compared to state we would like to be in, we can shift between the states more consciously. The two states below the line represent the victim state of life happening *to me* and the creator state of life happening *by me.* While in these two below-the-line states, we are typically closed, defensive, and committed to being right. The two states above the line represent the cocreator state where life happens *through me* and the at-one-with-all state where life happens *as me*. While being in the states above the line, we are open, curious, and committed to learning. Living mindfully, conscious of these states of being, enables us to ask ourselves whether we are operating above or below the line.

Dethmer and his coauthors provide excellent examples of the four ways of leading. They suggest that leaders operating in the To Me quadrant function as victims "at the effect of" something they consider outside of their control, such as external market forces, competitors, suppliers, family, finances, their health, their mood, to name a few. Something is wrong, and someone is to blame. Leaders operating in the By Me quadrant recognize there are skills and techniques to master in order to be an effective leader and have a curiosity as we explored in the conscious leadership practice of learning relentlessly. Dethmer et al. suggest that leaders are well served by focusing on the shift from To Me to By Me, from living in victim consciousness to living in creator consciousness, from being "at the effect of" to "consciously creating with." By Me leaders are purpose driven. Above the line, in the Through Me quadrant, leaders begin to shift from being controlling and leader centric to a place of surrender and letting go, where cocreation occurs without the need to be in control. Although still purpose driven, leaders look for a higher purpose to allow emergence through them rather than by them. Leaders truly operating in the As Me quadrant are hard to find but may be considered as being in a place of oneness and with an absence of self. The ten practices of conscious leadership will help most with the shift from the To Me to the By Me and Through Me quadrants.

Many of us spend much of our time in the To Me victim state of consciousness where life is hard, there is never enough of what we want, threats are constantly present, and we look to the past to assign blame. Victimhood is often illustrated using the drama triangle, originally introduced by Stephen Karpman in 1968 with the analysis of three fairy tales and the roles of persecutor, rescuer, and victim.[59] With the focus on victimhood, the shifting between roles is often overlooked, but Karpman's analysis of fairy tales is revealing. In his first analysis of the tale of the Pied Piper, "the hero begins as Rescuer of the city and Persecutor of the rats, then becomes Victim to the Persecutor mayor's double-cross, and in revenge switches to the Persecutor of the city's children. The mayor switches from Victim (of rats), to Rescuer (hiring the Pied Piper), to Persecutor (double-cross), to Victim (his children dead). The children switch from Persecuted Victims to Rescued Victims, to Victims Persecuted by their Rescuer." Taking a walk with David Emerald, storyteller in the *Power of Ted*, explains the role of victim when other people or situations are acting upon the individual, the role of persecutor or perpetuator and the perceived cause of the victim's woes, and the rescuer as the one who intervenes on behalf of the victim to save them from the prosecutor.[60] Although the rescuer may initially be seen to help the persecuted victim, feeling good about helping, and the victim feels the benefit, ultimately the rescuer, not feeling appreciated, may give up and become the victim persecuted by the original victim. The original persecutor may then show up as the rescuer. This drama plays out frequently in our interactions. Each of us has a more natural role, a starting place in each of the triangles—how we identify ourselves—but at some stage we are likely to end up feeling like the victim and maybe start thinking about how to get out of this drama triangle.

David Emerald,[61] Nilima Bhat and Raj Sisodia,[62] and the Conscious Leadership Group,[63] each describe shifts from the victim orientation to a creator orientation, where the role of the victim comes the role of creator, the role of persecutor becomes the role of challenger, and role of rescuer becomes the role of teacher or coach. Being mindful of these roles and potential shifts can help us move from the drama triangle to the presence triangle.

PRACTICING MINDFULNESS EVERY DAY

Becoming more conscious of our character and presence, of how to lead from above the line more often, and shifting away from the drama triangle requires us to live mindfully, practicing mindfulness every day. This can take the form of increased concentration, or allowing time for contemplation and reflection, or a more disciplined daily meditation practice.

Mindfulness teachers often refer to the power of the purposeful pause. David Steindl-Rast said, "Try pausing right before and right after undertaking a new action, even something simple like putting a key in a lock to open a door. Such pauses take a brief moment, yet they have the effect of decompressing time and centering you." A purposeful pause creates the space for being in the present moment before taking action or speaking to another person. Arthur Rubinstein, one of the greatest piano virtuosi, is reported to have said, "I handle notes no better than many others, but the pauses, ah, that is where the art resides." The simple pause, an extra breath, a look into the other person's eyes can all bring us into the present moment and allow us to really notice what is going on.

The purposeful pause creates the space for concentration. As we have already seen, we can be easily distracted. Concentration, with our high levels of distractibility, is a difficult practice. Erich Fromm, a German philosopher, suggests that the most important step in learning concentration is to learn to be alone with oneself.[64] Published more than sixty years ago, Fromm's *Art of Loving* describes living fully in the present, in the here and now, not thinking of the next thing to be done. Were this book to be written today, we may find the word *concentration* replaced by the word *mindfulness*, and although they are related, they are subtly different practices. Concentration seems to be a more intense style of mindfulness, a single-minded attentiveness to oneself and the task at hand with perhaps less attention on what is going on inside and around us.

Although meditation is becoming a more accepted practice in our lives and in business, some prefer the words contemplation, reflection, or prayer. Michael Carroll suggests when we think of contemplation, images of cloistered monks and nuns silently moving about the shadows of a monastery may come to mind, but he goes on to introduce broader possibilities for mindful leaders, defining contemplation as "carefully and wisely observing from an open place."[65] Carroll's process of contemplation is (1) rest the mind in the present moment, (2) shift to contemplation, (3) actively consider the object, (4) permit insight to touch the heart, (5) conclude with an aspiration, and (6) own the experience. Contemplative study enables active concentration and may include a call to action or at least an aspiration.

Chris Laszlo and his research team at Case Western Reserve University's Weatherhead School of Management identified reflective practices that support a flourishing enterprise and included meditation, journaling, immersion in nature, engaging with art, music, poetry, or literature, and less well-known powerful practices such as remembrance, transformational problem-solving, the highest goal exercise, and spiritual intelligence.[66] All of these practices increase our self-awareness and self-knowledge and create spaces for mindfulness that can lead us to consider taking early, sometimes difficult steps toward responsible action. Poet David Whyte reminds us to "Start close in, don't take the second step or the third, start with the first thing close in, the step you don't want to take."[67] Sometimes, the first step is the most difficult, but following our own voice, knowing what we stand for, gives us the courage to move. These reflective practices create valuable space for mindfulness, but without responsible action, they are only part of the journey. Laszlo's exploration of foundational individual practices, team and organizational practices, and systems-level practices are beyond the scope of this book but worthy of further investigation.

Many books have been dedicated to the practice of mindful meditation, and many of you reading this book may already have a meditation practice. My first experience of meditation was a guided visualization during a Creative Solutions Course at the Vanderbilt Hotel in London, more than thirty years ago. Strangely, despite numerous relocations and multiple archival downsizings, I kept the notes from that course. More importantly, the space for creativity that I established in my mind during that guided visualization is as vivid today as it was then. The board of advisors that I bring into that mind space has expanded, and as I prepared to write this book, I found the place getting a little overcrowded, but I've long appreciated the value of guided meditations. Since that first introduction to meditation, I have experienced numerous forms and styles of meditation and continue to explore the different meditation practices with curiosity and an open mind.

Getting to the cushion physically to sit in mindful meditation is not easy. In my Florida apartment, space is at a premium, and my *zabuton* (flat mat) and *zafu* (round cushion) are currently in storage. The physical cushion is no longer a requirement for my mindfulness practice; getting to the cushion has become the metaphor for creating the space for becoming mindful at any time in any place.

Sitting is a simple practice: sit on a cushion if you have one or, if not, on the floor or in a chair, sitting up straight and paying attention to the present moment, noticing what is going on. Teachers advocate different forms of breathing: five deep breaths, or the four-by-four technique of four breaths each with a four-second inhale, a four-second hold, a four-second exhale, and another four-second hold. I like the initial deep breaths followed by a return to more natural rhythmic breathing. This focus on the breath is the basis of most meditation techniques, but we all experience mind-wandering to a greater or lesser degree.

This mind-wandering is a critical aspect of living mindfully, noticing what is going on inside of us and also outside, beyond our thoughts. So, in your meditation practice, notice these thoughts, acknowledge them as thoughts, and return attention to the breathing. Avoid extending the narrative into a story and letting your mind wander too far. The inclusive practice of noticing what is going on provides a foundation for other conscious leadership practices.

Mindfulness is gaining wider recognition and acceptance in the business arena as a way to increase employee well-being and enhance collaboration, innovation, and leadership effectiveness. Research into mindfulness in the workplace is increasingly finding positive relationships between mindfulness and employee satisfaction, employee engagement, individual and team performance, and work-related wellbeing.[68, 69] Mindfulness practices can reduce work-related stress and the toxicity in the workplace described in later in this book. Mindful leadership and the practice of leading mindfully is an essential feature of conscious leadership that may be thought of as mindfulness with intention and responsible action.

Mindfulness creates the space for awareness, for noticing what is going on within us and around us. Living mindfully helps us avoid burnout, encourages self-compassion, and creates the space and time for rest and renewal. We can become more mindful of our energy depletion by looking at where we may be failing to meet our commitments. Renewal is about taking time to replenish our energy, refreshing ourselves and allowing us to be more mindfully engaged with physical energy, emotional connection, mental agility, and spiritual alignment with our higher purpose. Awareness of self, awareness of others, and awareness of the environment around us can all be enhanced by living mindfully, practicing mindfulness every day. With this increased attention, we can move on to setting intention and acting responsibly.

NOTICING WHAT IS GOING ON—LIVING MINDFULLY

Conscious Leadership Behaviors:

- Practicing mindfulness every day
- Being fully present to the current situation
- Being attentive to who we are and how we show up—our character and presence
- Finding our voice, performing authentically, being the best we can be
- Living mindfully in the moment, not replaying the past or anticipating the future
- Closing the gap between simple awareness and living mindfully
- Leading from above the line
- Shifting out of the drama triangle
- Practicing the purposeful pause
- Honoring opportunities for rest and renewal

PART II

Setting Intention

CHAPTER 4

Exploring Purposefully

Start with why. Simon Sinek, inspirational speaker and author, has been advocating this starting point in articles, books, and conversations for ten years, and there are an increasing number of leaders and organizations who now start with why. Individuals can usually describe *what* they and their organizations do, and many can describe *how* they do it, but, as Sinek asserts, very few people, including organizational leaders, can clearly articulate *why* they do *what* they do.[70] Purpose is the why—why we do what we do as individuals and organizations. Exploring purposefully with a possibility mindset, before committing to action, is an important practice for conscious leaders to apply in the process of setting intention.

The terms *purpose, mission,* and *vision* are often used interchangeably, but it is useful to maintain a distinction between these three terms. Purpose refers to the difference one wants to make in the world, mission is the core strategy that must be undertaken to fulfill that purpose, and vision is a vivid, imaginative description of how the world will look once that purpose has been realized. As I shared in the previous chapter, a major milestone in my journey through life was the inventure in East Africa led by Richard Leider, where the adventure of a walking safari across the Serengeti was combined with an inner journey of discovery. Leider, a pioneer in the world of purpose, describes purpose as an expression of the deepest dimension within us—of our central core or essence, where we have a profound sense of who we are, where we came from, and where we are going; purpose is what gives life meaning, your reason for being, your reason for getting up in the morning.[71] Some believe we are born with a calling. I am not so sure about that, but I do know our purpose is there; all we must do is discover it. Our purpose is what we say it is.

INDIVIDUAL PURPOSE

Although my inventure with Richard Leider was a major milestone and an incredible learning journey, my initial purpose-discovery experiences happened during a coaching relationship with Alan Seale, author of *Soul Mission, Life Vision*, in which he says your soul mission is your reason for being, your life purpose, your fundamental reason for doing what you do.[72] On the business card for my hot-air ballooning rides operation, I had written the tagline *taking people higher*. During our coaching conversations, I was able to discover and write down a life purpose statement based on a realization that my passion for ballooning was a manifestation of a much larger purpose. I discovered my purpose was *taking people higher, in business, in spirit, and in life*. In some ways, I hope this book will provide a sense of fulfillment aligned with that purpose. At least I was able to take my coach and his partner higher on a balloon ride over New York's Hudson Valley.

Uncovering your life purpose is an ongoing process of discovery. Noticing what occupies your mind and asking why are two places to start this journey of discovery, recommended by Roy Spence, one of the heroes of conscious capitalism, cofounder of the Purpose Institute, and author of *It's Not What You Sell, It's What You Stand For*.[73] Spence writes that the thoughts pervading your head may provide insights and signals to finding what you are passionate about, and where you may discover your purpose. In the first part of this book on conscious leadership, we focused on noticing what is going on within ourselves, with others, and with the environment around us. Putting our attention on the thoughts that pervade our minds while doing our daily work, during those moments of mindfulness or during wakeful periods before dropping off to sleep, during the middle of the night or those first moments of wakefulness in the morning, may point to what we are deeply passionate about and get us on the road to our purpose-discovery journey. Reflecting on a time when we felt truly passionate about what we have been doing or really fulfilled by what we accomplished is another way to begin to uncover what is important to us.

Questions we might ask during our purpose-discovery journey might include:

- Why do I do what I do?
- Why do I pursue the work life I do?
- Why is what I do worth doing?
- What issues, interests, causes, or challenges generate genuine enthusiasm?
- What energizes me the most?
- What am I passionate about?
- What keeps me up at night?
- What gets me up in the morning?
- What are my gifts?
- What do I truly believe in?
- What do I stand for?
- What is the legacy I want to leave behind?

As answers emerge, write them down. Identify the key phrases that resonate and bring energy and vitality into your being. Even when you have written something down that resonates, clarity of purpose may take time to emerge, and changes in the specific wording are not uncommon. Once purpose becomes clear, it can drive everything you do, and suddenly the seemingly impossible becomes possible.

In my coaching with clients who are Too Young to Retire® and in transition to the second half of life or the third age, I have found inspiration in the stories of the Purpose Prize winners. The prize was founded in 2005 by Marc Freedman, CEO of Encore.org. Since that time, the Purpose Prize has generated nearly ten thousand nominations and produced more than five hundred winners and fellows. The program has now transitioned to a new home at AARP.[74] The AARP Purpose Prize™ award honors extraordinary individuals who use their life experience to make a better future for all. For example, these award winners have been recognized for creating safe spaces for young people to escape from street violence and neighborhood gangs by blending music, dance, drama, and leadership; helping children and seniors with disabilities; and being a voice for an underserved, underrepresented population without a voice. Making a difference doesn't stop as you age. Millions of older adults are using their experience to give back, to solve problems, and to change lives. People all over the world are discovering their true purpose in encore careers that are making a difference for the young and the old, the underserved, in social justice, and in causes relating to many areas of our environment and the world around us.

Although many consider the pursuit of happiness to be an important part of any purpose or mission, happiness represents a desirable end state rather than a reason for being. As Viktor Frankl wrote in the preface to *Man's Search for Meaning*, "Don't aim at success—the more you aim at it and make it a target, the more you are going to miss it. For success, like happiness, cannot be pursued; it must ensue, and it only does so as the unintended side effect of one's personal dedication to a cause greater than oneself."[75] Happiness ensues as the result of living a life of meaning and purpose. Living purposefully may be fulfilling but may not make you happy all the time. I was always grateful for the happy, smiling faces of balloon passengers after a beautiful balloon ride, for people who helped me fulfill my purpose, but I was rarely happy jumping out of bed at three o'clock in the morning to check the weather and prepare for an early-morning sunrise flight.

Once you have your personal core purpose defined, you can begin to think about your organization's purpose. Robert Frost, in his poem, "Two Tramps in Mud Time," put it best: "My object in living is to unite, my avocation and my vocation, as my two eyes make one in sight." Combining your avocation (your personal purpose, what you want to do) with your vocation, (what you are paid to do) is surely a worthwhile objective.

ORGANIZATIONAL PURPOSE

It is said that organizations don't change, people do. Similarly, it is the people in organizations who define organizational purpose. Considering an organization as an organized body of individual people allows us to consider organizational purpose. In the same way as individual purpose is an individual's fundamental reason for being, the organizational core purpose is the organization's fundamental reason for being. Roy Spence suggests that an effective purpose is a definitive statement about the difference you want to make in the world and reflects the importance people attach to the company's work. It taps into their idealistic motivations and gets at the deeper reasons for an organization's existence beyond making money.[76] By the time you read this book, the leadership, ownership, and even the very existence of the specific, purposeful organizations I've included here may have changed. With that disclaimer, I have used a few organizations as exemplars in the area of organizational purpose with reference to individuals who, regardless of where they are organizationally as you read this book, are still likely to be great examples of purpose-driven leaders. Additional examples of conscious organizations can be found in chapter 10.

PATAGONIA

Bridging personal and organizational purpose when you are the founder or most senior leader may be easier than for the lower-level employee, but it is still not easy. Yvon Chouinard is founder and owner of Patagonia, a supplier of environmentally friendly clothes and equipment for silent sports, none of which require a motor and where reward comes in moments of connection between people and nature. In his book, *Let My People Go Surfing*, Chouinard explained why he was in business: "True, I wanted to give money to environmental causes. But even more, I wanted to create in Patagonia a model other businesses could look to in their own searches for environmental stewardship and sustainability, just as our pitons and ice axes were models for other equipment manufacturers." This purpose is supported by Patagonia's mission statement, "Build the best product, cause no unnecessary harm, use business to inspire and implement solutions to the environmental crisis."[77] Building the best product while at the same time doing no harm creates an interesting tension and, although not always possible to achieve, is a wonderful aspiration. Patagonia hire slowly, treat employees right, and train them to treat others right. Employees are often true Patagonia customers, spend time at play and in nature, and have a commitment to environmentalism along with an aversion to unconscious material consumption.

CONNER PARTNERS

The founders of Conner Partners concluded that a crucial answer to the question "Why are we here?" was "We are here to serve." Four main constituents of the purpose of service were identified as ourselves, our culture, our clients, and our communities, presented in an intentional sequence. Being aware of the flight safety preflight announcement to put oxygen masks on ourselves first before attending to children is a reminder that we can't properly attend to others unless we first take care of ourselves. It then follows that contributing to the communities where we conduct business is only possible if our clients have been adequately served and we as a firm have profits we can allocate for this purpose. This means all four of the primary constituencies are interdependent, but there is a preferred sequence in terms of where and when emphasis is placed on attending to needs. Healthy consultants are a prerequisite for a healthy firm, which is a prerequisite for healthy clients, which in turn is a prerequisite for the healthy communities we seek to serve.

MENTAL HEALTH ASSOCIATION OF PALM BEACH COUNTY

This is another personal example of organizational purpose—a not-for-profit social impact agency in the city where I have my Florida apartment. I serve on the board of directors. The focus of this mental health organization is to provide access to information and programs that promote mental wellness through advocacy, education, and outreach. Its purpose is described as *improving the lives of people touched by mental illness*. This is closely aligned with the individual purpose of the recently retired chief executive officer.

BARRY-WEHMILLER

With a similar theme, Bob Chapman, CEO of Barry-Wehmiller, says of his company, "Barry-Wehmiller is in business to improve lives. ... We are in business so that all our team members have meaningful and fulfilling lives." In his book *Everybody Matters*, coauthored with Raj Sisodia, Chapman talks about operating with a sense of profound responsibility for the lives entrusted to them and recognizing that everyone is important and worthy of care. The company has guiding principles of leadership that include "we measure success by the way we touch the lives of people."[78] The common thread of each of these examples, and the examples of conscious business shared in chapter 10, is the focus on employees first. Conscious leaders lead organizations with a strong sense of purpose closely related to serving people.

In an organization without purpose, a declared reason for being, people have no idea why they are there and what they are really there to do. There may be a lot of activity and busy work, but it all seems disorganized and directionless. In a purpose-driven organization, the purpose is clear, and all activities are aligned to that purpose. Conscious leaders lead on purpose.

LEADING WITH PURPOSE

My research in preparation for writing this book led me to an unusual source, a book unlikely to have found its way into my library in the normal course of events, yet a curious story about the search for meaning. Hermann Hesse, a German-born poet, novelist, and painter, and winner of the Nobel Prize in literature, wrote *Demian*, the story of Emil Sinclair's youth, during the first world war. Emil Sinclair's search for himself is a fascinating story, sounding both real and fictional simultaneously, and thought-provoking to say the least. One passage is worth sharing here:

> I did not exist to write poems, to preach sermons, to paint pictures; neither I nor anyone else existed for that purpose. All of that merely happened to a person along the way. Everyone had only one true vocation: to find himself. Let him wind up as poet or madman, as a prophet or a criminal—that wasn't his business; in the long run it was irrelevant. His business was to discover his own destiny, not just any destiny, and live it out totally and undividedly. Anything else was just a half measure, an attempt to run away, and escape back to the ideal of the masses, and adaptation, fear of one's own nature. Fearsome and sacred, the new image rose up before me; I had sensed it a hundred times, perhaps I had already enunciated it, but now I was experiencing it for the first time. I was a gamble of Nature, a throw of the dice into an uncertain realm,

leading perhaps to something new, perhaps to nothing; and to let this throw from the primordial depths take effect, to feel its will inside myself and adopt it completely as my own will: that alone was my vocation. That alone![79]

Only one genuine vocation, to find the way to ourselves; an experiment of nature, perhaps for a new purpose, perhaps for nothing. As we have seen in a previous chapter, our inner journey, our inner search for meaning, is often triggered by unexpected events and leads us in many directions. Being open to what is emerging on this journey may allow us to discover our true purpose. In any case, putting our perceived purpose into words is not enough. Experiencing and leading from this place helps us live purposeful lives and to lead purposefully—living and leading on purpose.

Following our true purpose, we can turn our work life into our life's work, our vocation into our avocation. This can be most fulfilling because it is done to make a difference in the world and for the people we serve rather than for personal recognition or financial reward. The power of purpose cannot be overstated. Purpose will drive everything, if we let it. If we look at our intentions, directions, strategies, and everyday decisions through the lens of our purpose, leading on purpose becomes easier. Exploring purposefully can make the seemingly impossible possible.

SETTING INTENTION—EXPLORING PURPOSEFULLY

Conscious Leadership Behaviors:

- Exploring inner places in the search for purpose and meaning
- Traveling purposefully on a journey of self-discovery
- Describing an individual core purpose in ten words or less
- Having an organizational purpose focused on people
- Aligning vocation with avocation
- Leading purposefully
- Living life on purpose
- Being passionate about exploring opportunities aligned to purpose
- Setting intentions and making decisions aligned to purpose
- Making the seemingly impossible possible

CHAPTER 5

Thinking Possibility

Having a purpose that makes the seemingly impossible possible can be enhanced by thinking and leading from a place of possibility rather than scarcity. Believing in multiple right answers, shifting from unconsciously limiting beliefs to consciously positive beliefs, linking generosity and possibility, and envisioning a future full of possibility are all features of the Thinking Possibility practice explored in this chapter. One of my favorite possibility thinkers is the White Queen in Lewis Carroll's *Through the Looking Glass and What Alice Found There*. The Queen, in response to Alice's skepticism about believing impossible things, suggested that Alice hadn't had enough practice and cited her own experience of practicing for half an hour a day and sometimes believing as many as six impossible things before breakfast. Although fictional, this children's story is a wonderful inspiration for possibility thinking. Thinking from a place of possibility can provide the bridge from a clearly defined purpose to committing to responsible action.

The *Power of Positive Thinking*,[80] written by Norman Vincent Peale, author, minister, and founder of the Guideposts organization, was first published in the year I was born. This practical guide to mastering the problems of everyday living is still in print today, more than sixty years later. The first chapter, "Believe in Yourself," aligns with my own philosophy that it all starts with belief. Belief in the possibility of realizing our dreams and intentions and achieving the seemingly impossible. Another possibility thinker, Ben Zander, conductor of the Boston Philharmonic Orchestra and co-author of *The Art of Possibility*, tells the story of the two salesmen who traveled to Africa in the 1900s. They were sent to find out if there was any opportunity for selling shoes, and they wrote telegrams back to

Manchester, England. One of them wrote, "Situation hopeless. They don't wear shoes." And the other one wrote, "Glorious opportunity. They don't have any shoes yet."[81]

Conscious leaders are possibility thinkers. They don't come from a place of scarcity, where there is never enough: never enough resources, never enough talented people, never enough money, never enough time. I'm sure you can add a few more "never enough" scarcity concerns of your own. Brené Brown,[82] research professor and best-selling author, in her analysis of the source of scarcity, suggests that the feeling of scarcity thrives in our shame-prone cultures that are deeply steeped in comparison and fractured by disengagement. She goes on to say that the counter approach to living in scarcity is not about abundance or more than you could ever imagine. Brown suggests that the opposite of scarcity is enoughness, built by wholeheartedness, vulnerability, and worthiness. Possibility thinkers have shifted from scarcity to sufficiency, from a place of never enough to a belief that there will always be enough. Conscious leaders embrace a belief in unlimited possibilities.

MULTIPLE RIGHT ANSWERS

I embraced the concept of multiple right answers after listening to Dewitt Jones, a National Geographic photographer, talk about his approach to taking photographs.[83] He recognized the paradigm we live in, a world based on fear, scarcity, and competition, which, Jones says, is only true if we choose to believe it, and that wasn't what nature was saying: Nature never stood in front of a forest and said, "There is one great photograph hidden here. One photographer will find it, and the rest of you will be hopeless losers." This was before the advent of digital cameras, and so nature said, "How many rolls [of film] you got, Dewitt? Bring it on. I'll fill them up. I'll fill them up with layers of beauty and possibility beyond anything you've ever imagined. Right down to my tiniest seed." In celebrating what is right with the world, we can build a vision of possibility, not scarcity. Possibility means there is always another right answer; it is a focus on what is right with the situation rather than what is wrong. Conscious leaders get contagiously excited and enthusiastic about future possibilities, striving to be the best *for* the world rather than the best *in* the world.

If you have read this book from the beginning, you'll already know of my interest in hot-air ballooning. I never set out to become a hot-air balloon pilot, and the purchase of my first hot-air balloon with three balloon group partners was more a result of typical English rainy weather than any intention to fly balloons. However, after an early promotion into a management role, my boss at the time inspired a philosophy of *do something different* and becoming a balloon pilot was certainly something very different from my other sporting adventures.

To take people higher in a hot-air balloon, we need calm winds and good visibility. For the sunrise flights, we often experience perfect conditions: light winds and, once the sun comes up and the fog burns off, excellent visibility. The sunset flights are more challenging. The late-afternoon winds often die down with the setting of the sun, by which time there is insufficient daylight left for a balloon flight. One of my favorite pictures of my balloon in flight shows the sun already set and me still in the air, virtually becalmed over trees. On this particular flight in New York's Hudson Valley, one of my passengers was a wonderful lady carrying her oxygen bottle who told me she was seventy-six years old! After about an hour, with the sun already set and virtually calm winds, we were floating very gently toward a small backyard surrounded by trees. Each time I allowed the balloon to descend, the trees acted like a magnet to the balloon; ascending to avoid the trees took us above the roof of the house, descending took us back toward the trees. Giving up on this small backyard and flying on was no longer an option. With darkness approaching and precious cargo on board, this was one of the days when I was in the air wishing I was on the ground rather than on the ground wishing I was in the air. It was imperative we land in this backyard. Fortunately, after a few aborted attempts, the chase crew arrived, and with a drop line and careful maneuvering, we landed safely on the tiny back lawn.

There are days when the weather is worse than the forecast, and we have to abort the idea of a free flight altogether and cancel the eagerly anticipated balloon ride. I can see the late change in the weather as a personal frustration and a disappointment for the passengers, spectators, and crew, but can I see the possibility in the situation? I avoid launching the balloon too close to sunset and risk landing in the dark, but what is the possibility here? So long as the balloon is tethered to the ground, I don't need the sunlight to find a place to land. I can inflate the balloon, anchor it to vehicles or trees, and give short, tethered rides to treetop height as long as the fuel and light allows. Instead of taking four people for a balloon ride, I can take fifty people on short, tethered rides. I am taking more people higher and, for many, fulfilling their dreams. On these occasions, I am thinking possibility; what is possible with the situation, not what is impossible. Ballooning in England, we might have rain where even a tethered ride is not possible. Then we can look for a country pub. More possibilities, more right answers.

The universe of possibility described by Ros and Benjamin Zander in *The Art of Possibility*, embraces the idea of generosity where action "may be characterized as generative, or giving, in all senses of that word, producing new life, creating new ideas, consciously endowing with meaning, contributing, yielding to the power of contexts."[84] Possibility and generosity are inextricably linked. The legendary story of the woman and the stone illustrates this relationship perfectly.

> *A wise woman was traveling in the mountains and found a precious stone in a stream. The next day, she met another traveler who was hungry, and the wise woman opened her bag to share her food. The hungry traveler saw the precious stone and asked the woman to give it to him. She did so without hesitation. The traveler left, rejoicing his good fortune. He knew the stone was worth enough to give him security for a lifetime. But a few days later, he came back to return the stone to the wise woman. "I've been thinking," he said. "I know how valuable the stone is, but I give it back in the hope that you can give me something even more precious: give me what you have within you that enabled you to give me the stone."*

What can become possible through our own generosity?

LEADING WITH POSSIBILITY

Many of us accept that there are things we cannot change, but rather than living our lives reacting to forces outside of our control, Joseph Jaworski, founder the American Leadership Forum and the Global Leadership Institute, proposed an alternative: if individuals and organizations operate from the generative orientation, from possibility rather than resignation, we can create the future into which we are living as opposed to merely reacting to it when we get there.[85] Showing up with this generative orientation is not simply a matter of switching the glass-half-empty negativity thinking to the glass-half-full thinking of possibility. It is about listening for what is wanting to emerge in the world, seeing the possibilities, and then having the courage to take responsible action.

This story of the two wolves may be familiar:

> *One evening a grandfather told his grandson about a battle that goes on inside people. He said, "My son, the battle is between two wolves inside us all. One is evil; it is anger, envy, jealousy, sorrow, regret, greed, arrogance, self-pity, guilt, resentment, inferiority. The other is good; it is joy, peace, love, hope, serenity, humility, kindness, benevolence, empathy, generosity, truth, compassion, and faith." The grandson thought about it for a minute and then asked his grandfather, "Which wolf wins?" The grandfather simply replied, "The one you feed."*

Conscious leaders feed the good wolf.

The willingness to consider possibility requires a tolerance of uncertainty and an acceptance of ambiguity and even confusion at times. My own academic journey began inauspiciously enough with mediocre performance at school and an initial apprenticeship as an engineering technician, following in the footsteps of my paternal grandfather who, for many years, was a mechanical fitter in the Naval Dockyards in southern England. After a couple of years, I could see the possibility that, with a little extra effort, I would have the prerequisites to shift gears and study for a mechanical engineering degree at the local polytechnic. The company where I was employed as a technician apprentice supported my aspirations and agreed to sponsor my four-year degree program. As I mentioned earlier in the book, when I informed my father of my plans, he began questioning my ability to successfully complete the degree program. He was in effect asking the question, "Do you think you are good enough?" This wasn't the only time he had asked that question, and the fear of not being good enough has haunted me since early childhood. He never stopped asking the question, but after three postgraduate degrees, we both gained a better perspective of the answer.

My father, in passing on his own fear of failure to me, raised my own level of uncertainty about the likelihood of success. The possibility of graduating with a degree in mechanical engineering was based more on an aspirational dream than a foundation of academic success, and completion was in no way a certainty. Yet I believed it was possible, and despite life-changing challenges during the first academic year, I successfully graduated four years later. Since then, I have attempted to balance the fear of not being good enough with the mantra "dream big." Big dreams open doors to possibility thinking.

Big dreams may allow for possibility thinking, but, as was written on the wall of our Quest Worldwide office in New Jersey, it all starts with belief. Our beliefs create our reality and act as lenses or filters through which we see either possibilities or hopelessness. What we believe enables or inhibits our possibility thinking. Kevin Cashman, author of *Leadership from the Inside Out*, describes two distinct types of belief systems: conscious beliefs (the explicit, known beliefs we have) and shadow beliefs (those that are secret, hidden, unexplored, or unresolved).[86] Not being good enough was one of my long-held shadow beliefs, and although it in some ways fueled a drive to succeed and prove my father wrong, an increasing awareness of this limiting belief has enabled a shift toward a conscious belief in what is possible and greater confidence in the likelihood of success.

Our beliefs influence our thoughts, which in turn determine our behaviors. Although the idea that *thoughts become things* and *what we think about we bring about* was made popular by the book and video *The Secret*, writing about thoughts becoming things dates back to before my grandparents were born. Prentice Mulford, the nineteenth-century new-thought pioneer, first published his inspirational essays, *Thoughts are*

Things, in 1889. In one of his essays, Mulford writes about looking forward, noting that although one chief characteristic of the material mind is to hold tenaciously to the past, power comes from looking forward with hope, of expecting and demanding the better things to come.[87] This is the law of the infinite mind, and when we follow it, we live in that mind, a mind that believes in possibilities and multiple right answers.

Shifting the shadow or limiting beliefs into more consciously positive beliefs is crucial to being able to lead with possibility. Lion Goodman, creator of the Belief Closet process, suggests that beliefs are like old computer programs—once they are programmed into us, they continue to operate in the background forever. The good news is, it is possible to delete those old useless programs through a process of conscious identification and choice. Goodman's Belief Closet process helps remove or reprogram these limiting beliefs.[88] Uncovering and understanding potentially limiting beliefs allows us to create new conscious beliefs to replace those limiting beliefs. More than simply affirmations, this process for clearing limited beliefs helps create consciously positive beliefs that enable possibility thinking. One of the tools I like to use in clearing limiting beliefs is to go to the worst-case scenario method and ask the question, "What is the worst that can happen?" Then consider what do you need to do to minimize the risks associated with that worst-case scenario. Becoming conscious of our beliefs, clearing limiting beliefs, and creating beliefs that enable possibility thinking are prerequisites to leading with possibility.

Returning to the fear of not being good enough that was instilled by my father, and my ensuing motivation to complete my degree, I am reminded of Lance Secretan's distinction between inspiration and motivation. He suggests that motivation is extrinsic, something we do to people, and comes from a combination of fear and material rewards or punishments. Inspiration is intrinsic, coming not from fear but from love; motivation is based on a need for each other, inspiration is based on love for each other.[89] As my father aged, he became more inspirational than motivational, and during his final few months of life, I needed no motivation for the frequent trips across the Atlantic to care for him. The last time I saw him, a few hours before his death, his mind already failing, he asked where my mother was. His wife for sixty-six years had predeceased him by a few months, and he was ready to join her. I learned a lot about love from both of them and appreciated their possibility thinking.

Ben Zander realized his job as a conductor was to awaken possibility in other people. He suggests speaking in possibility springs from an appreciation that what we say creates a reality, that how we define things sets a framework for life to unfold. He asks us to imagine prefacing our remarks with the immortal words of Martin Luther King Jr.: "I have a dream ..." A dream can be the beginning of possibility thinking.

Speaking in possibility is a conscious leadership behavior.

ENVISIONING THE FUTURE

With awareness, purpose, courage, and possibility thinking, conscious leaders can envision and describe a desired future state for themselves and their organizations and begin to enroll others in their vision. When I joined strategy execution consulting firm Conner Partners, I was given the title *intent architect*. An architect, in its classic definition, designs structures with an intended purpose. Similar to these structural architects, the intent architect helps senior leaders envision, design, and build desired future states for their organizations—future states envisioned by senior leaders that enable realization of a major transformational change. The role of the intent architect was to help clients with a process of extracting, clarifying, and expressing the intent of a transformational change; ensuring understanding, alignment, and commitment of the senior leadership team to this intent; inspiring creativity and clarity during the design of a solution to achieve the desired future state; and ensuring realization of the intent of a major organizational transformation. An essential output of this intent clarification process was a statement of intent that included the case for change, desired future state, realization indicators, and guiding principles for the change. A shared view of the essential elements of the desired future state was developed as a simple, bold, and inspiring illustration using both graphical expression and clear, compelling script—and able to be drawn on the "back of a napkin." For the conscious leader, this statement of intent— and more specifically the expression of the desired future state—embraces people, purpose, and presence as well as profit.

Envisioning a bold and inspiring future often requires leaders to work beyond both the boundaries of previous successes and the edges of their comfort zones. Judi Neal, founder of the Association for Spirit at Work, describes an "edgewalker" as a leader who has learned to walk in many different worlds without getting completely caught up in any one of them, someone who is able to walk the fine line between these worlds. Edgewalkers are the bridge builders who link different paradigms, cultural boundaries, and worldviews.[90] Edgewalker qualities are not unlike the qualities of a conscious leader—self-awareness, passion, integrity, vision, and playfulness. Leaders who walk on the edge are shapeshifters who can hold the attention of opposites or polarities and maintain an eye on the future, prepared to try what hasn't been tried before, trusting their intuition and breaking new ground. Conscious leaders take themselves to their edge, ready to jump off the cliff and prepared to learn to fly on the way down. In the words of writer T. S. Eliot, "Only those who will risk going too far can possibly find out how far one can go."

Courage is another characteristic of conscious leaders who can envision a bold and exciting future state. A carved ebony lion in a walking pose is an important symbol of courage I brought back with me from my inventure in East Africa. The lion has long been a symbol of courage, although, in the *Wizard of Oz*, the cowardly lion wished for courage, having lost it along the way. Mark Nepo, a writer and philosopher, reminds us that the journeys of facing the lion and being the lion are inescapable.[91] Being the lion, the symbol of courage, strength, and power, seems easy to comprehend, although, in the stories through the ages, we find both the lionhearted, energy filled and positive, along with the brutal and all-consuming king of the jungle. The conscious leader chooses to be the lion who is brave, determined, courageous, valiant, gallant, intrepid, bold, and daring rather than the lion who wants to be king of the jungle—controlling, dictatorial, autocratic, and overbearing. For conscious leaders, courage is not an excuse for impulsive or aggressive behavior but an opportunity to stand up for what we believe in.

Facing the lion refers to both our internal struggles as well as external challenges. Facing our internal struggles is an honest encounter with those inner demons that inhibit possibility thinking. This is an essential part of our inner journey. Confronting the external challenges that Nepo refers to as "facing the unleashed power of the lion run amok" requires us to take a stand, standing up to these challenges and to people who dishearten all they touch by their negative, impossibility thinking. Conscious leaders embrace the behaviors required for both being the lion and facing the lion.

Possibility thinking and living mindfully in the present moment may at first sight appear to be different polarities, as discussed in an earlier chapter describing the practice of learning relentlessly. We all tend to live to some degree in each of the past, the present, and the future perspectives. The past perspective represents a degree of certainty that something has happened in a particular way, enables learning, and helps us avoid making the same mistakes again. The present perspective is about living mindfully in the present moment, not being concerned about the past, which cannot be changed, and limiting our concern about the probability or likelihood of future events. The future perspective of possibility thinking enables us to look forward and embrace opportunities based on our dreams and aspirations. Considering these three perspectives as interdependent polarities helps us consciously select the perspective in which we are living at any moment without losing sight of the other two perspectives. Conscious leadership is about learning to shape the future from the perspective of generative, emerging, possibility thinking. I like to think of this as "shaping our future as if we will live forever yet living today as if we will die tomorrow."

A final word on possibility thinking from Wilferd Peterson, an author of inspirational essays: "Walk with the dreamers, the believers, the courageous, the cheerful, the planners, the doers, the successful people with their heads in the clouds and their feet on the ground. Let their spirit ignite a fire within you to leave this world better than when you found it."

SETTING INTENTION—THINKING POSSIBILITY

Conscious Leadership Behaviors:

- Considering multiple perspectives, multiple right answers
- Doing something radically different compared to what we have done in the past
- Focusing on sufficiency rather than scarcity
- Being contagiously excited and enthusiastic about future possibilities
- Reframing negative perspectives into positive, possibility thinking
- Envisioning a meaningful future for ourselves and our organizations
- Communicating a positive and hopeful outlook for the future
- Striving to be the best *for* the world rather than the best *in* the world
- Being an edgewalker, ready to jump off the cliff and learning to fly on the way down
- Walking with the dreamers, igniting the fire of possibility

CHAPTER 6

Committing to Action

Conscious leaders can articulate a compelling vision of the future aligned to purpose and passion and, with a strong personal commitment to responsible action, translate that vision into clearly stated goals and intentions that build understanding, alignment, and commitment in others. A personal purpose-driven vision and a personal commitment to responsible action are prerequisites for the development and realization of an organizational vision. In this chapter, we will explore the differences between *intentions* and *goals*, and between *realization* and *installation*, and begin building the bridge from *commitment* to *responsible action*.

INTENTIONS, GOALS, OUTCOMES, AND RESULTS

Although specific goals, outcomes, and desired results are essential for measuring personal and organizational transformations, conscious leaders place greater attention on their intentions. Establishing goals, outcomes, or desired results enables the focus on what we want to achieve. Intentions focus more on how we want to *be* during the journey toward the desired future state. Before writing this book, I defined, with the help of a book-writing coach, specific goals based on milestones along the development timeline, together with desired outcomes and results from writing and publishing the book. I also defined the benefits to the reader, the results I hope you will realize from learning about the practices described in this book. However, my intentions are more focused on the journey before, during, and after publication, reflecting how I show up as an author, teacher, and conscious leadership coach. My intentions as author and teacher are to show up in the book as inspirational, educational, instructive, thought provoking, practical, serious, and engaging. My intention as a conscious leadership coach is to show up in service to leaders who are seeking to lead more consciously and make a positive difference in the world. The realization of these intentions, while more difficult to measure than specific goals, outcomes, or results, will be known to the readers of this book and the clients in my conscious leadership coaching practice. With clear intentions, specific goals follow more easily.

The words *intent* and *intention* also share meanings and overlap in use, but they are not completely interchangeable. To reinforce the distinctions explored in the previous paragraph, let's consider the concept of the Commander's Intent in which US Marines identify two parts to a mission: the task, which is the action to be taken, and the intent, which is the desired result or outcome of the task.[92] The intent describes what must be achieved and typically includes purpose, objective, sequence of steps, rationale, key decisions, anti-goals, and possible constraints or limitations. The situation may change, making the task obsolete, but the intent is more permanent and continues to guide the actions being taken. The intention, or how the intent is achieved, is described as the philosophy of command and, for the US Marines, is based on decentralized command, where all leaders at all levels demonstrate sound and timely judgment; on exploiting human characteristics rather than relying on equipment and procedures; and on implicit communication with mutual understanding established through familiarity and trust built upon on shared philosophy and shared experience. Intention means having clarity about how we show up as leaders—our values and beliefs, our character and presence. Although clarity of intent is essential to strategy execution, the focus of the conscious leadership practices espoused in this book is on intentions more than intent.

In a similar distinction between outcomes and intentions, Fred Kofman, philosopher and vice president of leadership and organizational development at LinkedIn, compares the Olympic gold medalist as the event winner who achieves the desired outcome with the athletes who did not win but who were able to celebrate the effort and commitment and the process of competing.[93] I applaud those athletes with an intention of being the best they can be more than the win-at-all-costs athletes, many of whom appear to have relied on performance-enhancing substances and unethical behaviors. Kofman also reminds us of Maradona's "hand of God," which I remember all too well. During the 1986 FIFA World Cup soccer match between England and Argentina, Diego Maradona scored a goal using his hand. The referee thought he had used his head and allowed the goal to stand, and later Maradona claimed it was the hand of God. This lack of integrity is all too commonplace in the sporting world, as shown by the increasing evidence from instant video replays. This celebration of the results of cheating shows a lack of integrity based on the end justifying the means. Maradona's second goal that day was nothing short of brilliant and was acclaimed as the goal of the century, but for many, including all English soccer fans, Maradona will be remembered for his cheating and his apparent desire to win at all costs. Acting with integrity is another conscious leadership practice explored later in this book.

Returning to Mariana Bozesan's research into the "Integral Approach to the Making of a Consciousness Leader in Business," her findings show how research participants with a focus on intentions rather than outcomes achieve better results.[94] Through their transformation, the consciousness leaders participating in the research realized that they became even more successful if they let go of their goals, their need to control people and situations, and stopped working so hard. As a result, they learned to reduce their focus on their outcomes, life plans, and even personal careers. As they established intentions instead of outcomes, they became more open and were able to see more opportunities than before. By simply getting out of their own way, the universe constantly and positively surprised them with its potential. This focus on intention precedes rather than replaces a statement of intent, which, as we saw in the last chapter, might include the case for change, a compelling expression of the desired future state, desired realization outcomes, and principles for guiding the journey. In some ways, these guiding principles are not dissimilar to our intentions in that they inform and guide our decision-making.

Focusing on intentions does not mean you give up your goals or desire to achieve. Goals are important, usually external and focused on the future, with a specific destination or achievement in mind. Intentions are lived each day, in the present moment, independent of achieving the goal or destination, and reflect our inner relationships with ourselves and others. The more conscious we become, the more we crave alignment of what we say and do with who we are.

REALIZATION VERSUS INSTALLATION

In presenting ideas around intent, I have referred to realization outcomes. At Conner Partners, we made a clear distinction between realization and installation indicators, and this is worth explaining here. Research has shown that 70 percent of strategic change initiatives fail to produce their intended results. The reason for much of this failure is that organizations focus on installation rather than realization. Installation deals with managing the tangible, logistical aspects of introducing something new into the work environment (e.g., establishing new assignments, roles, or responsibilities; engaging new organizational structures; introducing hardware or software; training people; or scheduling events). As important as installation is to achieving ultimate goals, it becomes dysfunctional if it is viewed as an end state rather than a key step in moving toward solution realization. Realization occurs when an initiative has its full, intended impact on the ultimate desired outcome. Realization is about accomplishing what was originally promised when the money was allocated to build or buy the solution. It incorporates tangible indicators of success that lend themselves to quantification as well as more subjective but still measurable aspects of the solution's desired effect. Tools such as the balanced strategy and the balanced scorecard provide the basis for measuring both installation and realization. Although this is not a book about strategy execution, being conscious of this distinction between realization and installation and the need for alignment, engagement, and discipline is important for the conscious leader. The practices for leading consciously also encourage a shift from the world of measurement, where survival is often a primary issue, to a universe of possibility stretching beyond measurement to a world of opportunity, generativity, and sufficiency described in previous chapters.

THE BRIDGE FROM COMMITMENT TO ACTION

With a compelling statement of intent and clear intentions of how we wish to show up in the world, true commitment becomes a possibility. Several writers, including one of the great German literary figures Johann Wolfgang von Goethe, have been credited with the line, "Until one is committed, there is hesitancy, the chance to draw back." While the statement is partly true, there is a big difference between declaring commitment and being truly committed to our intentions and the goals for realizing the desired future state.

While attending a spiritual retreat a few years ago, I experienced one of those rare moments of real awakening. Despite being intensely goal driven at times, my awareness of a long-practiced habit of running away from situations was heightened dramatically during one of the meditative exercises. I suddenly realized the number of significant situations from which I had run away: I ran away from home; I ran away from the church that was an anchor during my formative years; I ran away from a failing marriage; I ran away from numerous jobs that had become unexciting. It was not always easy to leave, and in leaving somewhere, I was always heading toward another place, all too often without a true purpose other than getting away from a bad situation. Since then, I have developed a stronger commitment to running enthusiastically toward something rather than running fearfully away, and although still unconsciously running away from dark places, I now more consciously practice running toward the light. I declare my commitment to my intentions and goals. Feeling compelled to move forward rather than simply running away is a much more positive commitment to action.

Commitment is also a matter of contribution. Ben Zander, conductor of the Boston Philharmonic Orchestra, expresses similar thoughts about running away, thinking that nothing was ever quite good enough, even to the extent of considering there was always another orchestra aside from the one he was conducting that he suspected would bring him more success. In that regard, he never felt fully present on the conductor's podium.[95] Zander introduced a game called *I am a contribution*, replacing a childhood game with a question of "What did you achieve today?" with the question "How will I be a contribution today?" Zander suggests declaring yourself to be a contribution and throwing yourself into life as someone who makes a difference, accepting that you may not understand how or why but are ready serve and step boldly forward. Being a contribution goes beyond declaring a commitment to living a commitment.

Running toward rather than running away is not to say that we don't first have to let go of the past to embrace the future. The Transition Model, introduced by organizational consultant and author William Bridges, has three overlapping stages beginning with endings, transitioning through the neutral zone, to making a beginning.[96] I can recall numerous situations where I have begun moving forward with a new beginning only to find I wasn't ready to let go of the way things had been to make space for what might be wanting to emerge. My running away from home in my early teens was short-lived because I wasn't prepared to let go of the comforts of home. Even after declaring my intent to leave home, I was initially unwilling to make the supreme effort required. It wasn't until the pain of living in a highly restrictive religious environment became greater than the fear of the unknown world beyond that protective environment that I was able to begin the transition. I began work on endings, accepting that I would be cut off from family and friends who chose the exclusivity of their religious environment, and I began to look forward to new beginnings. The somewhat chaotic period of uncertainty in the neutral zone turned out to be relatively short-lived thanks to a few wonderful people who served as mentors and guides, although in some ways the transition process continues to this day. As those who have left similar restrictive religious environments will attest, letting go completely is not easy, but I was able to progress through the letting-go phase sufficiently to allow for new possibilities to emerge and for me to commit to a new life. As it turned out, I had committed to something larger than I had ever imagined, and through that commitment, as I have come to realize over time, I achieved a life of meaning and adventure I had never thought possible. This traumatic transition provided a foundation for many other major transitions in life and at work that have helped me empathize with clients experiencing personal and business transformations.

Turning to the commitment required for leaders of organizational transformations, we know that the primary reason organizational change initiatives fail to realize intended outcomes is ineffective sponsorship.

The sponsor is the leader who has the power to authorize or legitimize the change, the one person who can say go ahead or stop. Sponsorship is critical to successful change and cannot be delegated to subordinates or change agents. At Conner Partners, we defined the characteristics of effective sponsors as purposeful, attentive, committed, decisive, and resolute. Leaders who are fully committed to the realization of the intent of the change do the following:

- Publicly demonstrate the depth of their personal commitment to the endeavor
- Privately demonstrate personal commitment with behind-the-scenes actions that show they are not just paying lip service in public
- Communicate powerfully using clear, accurate, and compelling language to convince others that achieving realization is a business imperative
- Apply consequences, using positive and negative reinforcement to sanction change and drive tactical objectives as well as strategic goals
- Accept that effective sponsorship requires both an ongoing openness to new ways of thinking and behaving, and an appreciation for the importance of learning from mistakes

The change execution methodology at Conner Partners provided many opportunities and milestones for committing to action and, where necessary, for deciding to step back and not commit to implementation. Having clearly defined the intent of the change with a detailed transformation plan, we helped organizational leaders consider the impact of alternative plans such as accelerating implementation, decelerating implementation, and in rare but important cases, cancelling or redesigning the proposed organizational transformation. Effective change leaders demonstrate strong personal commitment for full realization of the intended outcomes but, without the effective commitment of their leadership teams, are unlikely to be successful. Effective change leaders build a strong network of sponsorship that extends down through the organization from the initiating sponsor to all primary sustaining and local sustaining sponsors.

This process of cascading sponsorship requires effective sponsorship at the highest level, with leaders inviting team members to take a seat on the bus. That seat is not guaranteed for all team members. The seat assignment must be earned with a demonstrated commitment to fulfill cascading sponsorship duties. To earn a seat on the bus, team members must do three things: (1) demonstrate sufficient understanding, alignment, and commitment, to start the journey; (2) recognize that it is impossible to be fully prepared at the point of getting on the bus; and (3) be ready to identify and close gaps that exist and accept that, as identified gaps are closed, new ones will surface that must also be addressed. This means the process of learning to be a better sponsor will continue throughout the transformation process. We encouraged a meeting with entire leadership teams to declare the commitment and demonstrate that they have individually earned the right to a seat on the bus. In major change initiatives, not everyone gets a seat, and many get off along the way.

Simply declaring commitment is not enough. Remember the story about the five frogs sitting on a log? Four decide to jump off. How many are left sitting on the log? You may at first think only one was left, but all five are likely still sitting on the log. Four *decided* to jump off, but we don't know about their level of commitment to *taking action*. We don't know if they jumped or not.

In *Managing at the Speed of Change*, Daryl Conner introduces the commitment curve which represents the stages of commitment to change.[97] Preparation, acceptance, and commitment represent three phases of progression along the commitment curve. Getting to even limited levels of commitment requires a progression through the first two phases. During the preparation phase, contact with and awareness of a change may result in confusion or, with increasing understanding, a crossing of the disposition threshold to the acceptance phase where, if a positive disposition ensues, we may pass into the commitment phase. A limited degree of commitment may encourage experimentation and even adoption. At any time before adoption, the change can be aborted. Even after adoption, the change can be terminated or, if successful, move on to the institutionalization and internalization phases. We can see that committing to action is not so much a binary choice but a process of increasing commitment that can be terminated at any stage. A multitude of other commitments can also affect the level of commitment we may or may not wish to make.

We all have competing commitments that may keep us from taking action. Professor Robert Kegan[98] describes the gap between a person's real intention to do something and what the person actually does. He provides an illustration in which heart doctors advised their patients to take their medications as prescribed or literally die. Follow-up research showed that only one out of seven actually took the prescribed medications. The other six had just as great a desire to stay alive but risked death by not following their doctor's advice. Kegan talks about the difference between a person's genuine intention and what the person is actually able to bring about. This is the challenge of competing commitments. These may be a matter of too many priorities, but Keegan suggests that thoughts and feelings reflect subconscious competing commitments that are thwarting a stated intention and may be a matter of self-delusion.

Keegan goes on to tell the story of a guy going into a bar every day after work and ordering three individual shot glasses of whiskey. He proceeds to slowly drink the three glasses of whiskey. Finally, the bartender says, "You know, I've been serving you these three glasses of whiskey for a while now, and I know it's none of my business, but I just have to ask. Why do you do this? We have bigger glasses, and I can pour you a triple in one glass." The guy says, "I'll explain it to you. A few years ago, my two brothers and I used to come here to this bar at the end of the day and each have a drink and chat about the activities of the day, but modern life being what it is, their work has taken them far away, one to Atlanta and the other to London, so we can't get together at the end of the day like we used to. So, what we each do is, at the end of the day in our respective time zones, we go to our favorite bar or a pub, and we each order the three separate glasses, and we reflect on the day and think about each other. It is a nice way for us to stay together, each knowing that the other two are doing the same thing." So, the bartender understood, and although he had never heard of such a thing before, it was okay, and he continued to set out the three glasses of whiskey. And then one day the guy came in and said, "Just two glasses today." The bartender was curious but didn't like to ask, so he gave him the two glasses of whiskey each day. In the end, curiosity got the better of the bartender, and he had to ask, "Why only two glasses?" And the guy looked at the bartender and said, "I've quit drinking!" Self-deception is a very powerful force in human affairs and may be a major factor in the failure to convert commitments into responsible action.

Committing to responsible action requires clarity about the intent of the change and our intention about the way we show up during the process of the realization of that intent. Declaring commitment is not enough. Conscious leaders are purpose-driven possibility thinkers who, once committed, can inspire others to join them on the journey to the desired future state. Patanjali, an Indian sage who is believed to have compiled the *Yoga Sutras*, put it this way:

> When you are inspired by some great purpose, some extraordinary project, all your thoughts break their bonds; your mind transcends limitation, your consciousness expands in every direction, and you find yourself in a new, great, and wonderful world. Dormant forces, faculties, and talents become alive and you discover yourself to be a greater person by far than you ever dreamed.

The bridge from commitment to acting responsibly is about our personal responsibility for making a positive difference in the world. Speaking candidly, acting with integrity, and taking responsible action are the conscious leadership practices for acting responsibly, which will be explored in the next section.

SETTING INTENTION—COMMITTING TO ACTION

Conscious Leadership Behaviors:

- Developing a compelling expression of the desired future state
- Running purposefully toward the desired future rather than away from past experiences
- Making clear distinctions between intent (the what) and intentions (the how)
- Describing clear intentions for the journey to future possibilities
- Declaring commitment to realization of the intended outcomes of the journey
- Recognizing and taking action to address competing commitments
- Building understanding, alignment, and commitment in others
- Craving alignment of who we are with what we say and do
- Being a contribution and making a difference
- Taking personal responsibility for converting commitment into responsible action

PART III

Acting Responsibly

CHAPTER 7

Speaking Candidly

The practices of acting responsibly are speaking candidly, acting with integrity, and taking responsible action. Speaking candidly requires us to be straightforward and unequivocal, speaking our truth quietly, delivering messages with clarity, respect, and kindness, and inspiring conversations that matter. This may require us to develop a different language, using different words than we have used before. After moving from England to the United States of America in the 1990s, I confirmed Winston Churchill's view of two countries divided by a common language. I found myself having to learn a new language using the same words, with minor differences in the spelling and significant differences in pronunciation. In addition to that, I became increasingly aware of the importance of words and of ensuring understanding of what important words mean. Building a personal relationship with a New Yorker from Long Island proved particularly challenging; clarifying what we each meant by the use of specific words became a common feature of our interactions.

Mealtimes were a major challenge, often beginning with the question, "Do you want chips with that?" In the US, we are familiar with potato chips or corn chips, but in England, famous for the gourmet meal of fish and chips, chips are what Americans call fries. We had to clarify what sort of chips were expected with a meal. Cookies in the US are biscuits in England. In the US, the first floor usually means the ground floor of a building, but in England, the first floor is the second floor or at least the floor above the ground floor. We confuse jumpers and sweaters, trousers and pants, trainers and sneakers, waistcoats and vests, braces and suspenders, to highlight just a few. For automobiles, I had to learn that the boot was now a trunk, and the bonnet was now a hood. I could go on. There are many other examples, some not fit for printing in a book about conscious leadership, but this serves to remind us of the importance of clarifying what important words mean and using them appropriately.

More important than simply understanding what words mean is how we use them and our tone of voice when communicating with others. Face-to-face and telephone interactions have been replaced in many cases by emails, texts, and instant messages where the tone of voice is lost, and misunderstandings occur easily. As we noted in the chapter on learning relentlessly, the brevity of the written communication and the inability to hear the tone of voice can cause significant, often unintended, reactions, and the desire to respond immediately with an angry reply-all message can be overwhelming. Speaking candidly when using the written word increases the risk of misunderstanding and requires us to write carefully and thoughtfully. In-person interactions are always preferred, and never more so than when we wish to be frank and straightforward. We will explore honesty and openness, kindness and compassion, concealing and revealing, building trust through our conversations, and conscious languaging in this chapter about speaking candidly.

HONESTY AND OPENNESS

Speaking honestly and openly is about truth telling, speaking your truth quietly and confidently, and being frank and straightforward. Speaking your truth, standing up for what you believe in, is about authentic or conscious communication, but it's not about being right, proving the other person wrong, or attributing blame. It is about helping others understand why you think the way you do. Fred Kofman uses the term "productive expression" as a way to effectively present viewpoints to others, in a way that helps to reveal and resolve differences by sharing information, objectives, and needs.[99] Guidelines for productive expression include finding common ground, providing facts, owning your opinions, recommending actions, ensuring comprehension, and accepting challenges. Speaking candidly also requires us to listen with all our senses.

At Conner Partners, we shared a commitment to developing strong partnerships with clients along with being viewed as a rare and valuable asset, as opposed to being just another vendor. What comes with being in partnership with clients is the obligation to be respectful and sensitive but always frank and straightforward about our views and recommendations. Being frank is being honest, sometimes in a blunt and antagonistic manner. Straightforward is being direct, getting directly to the point, without deviation. The effectiveness of being frank and straightforward depends on where we stand, from what place the communication emanates.

Bob Chapman tells the story about the US Air Force in his book *Everybody Matters*.[100] He describes a practice known as brutal honesty where, after a mission, people go into the debriefing room to tell the pilot everything he could have done better, in a very frank and straightforward manner. They hold nothing back and criticize every single thing the pilot may have done that was less than perfect. The intent, of course, is to create the finest flying force in the world to defend our freedom. They come from a place of perfection. But Bob asked one of the officers, "If that airman was your son, would you speak to him that way?" Without hesitating, the officer said, "No, of course not!" Bob's next question was, "If the pilot goes out and flies a mission the next day and nails it, getting everything right, would you say, 'Great Job. Well done!'?" The answer was "No. We don't have time to tell them what's right." Later in the day, the officer shared his aha moment. He had unwittingly been taking brutal honesty home and was being constantly critical of his young son. He said, "When I get home tonight, I am going to tell my eight-year-old son everything I like about him." How often do we take the rigor of military-style command and control environments, where there is a need for faultless performance delivered with precision and perfection, into a working environment where teamwork and collaboration are required for success, or into our family situations where we seek love and harmony? We need to be frank and straightforward, but we don't need the brutality.

Expressing ourselves honestly in any relationship is essential to our sense of well-being, but we need to come from a caring mindset. Subir Chowdhury, author of *The Difference*, suggests that a caring mindset requires us to be straightforward, thoughtful, and accountable, and to have resolve.[101] Being straightforward needs to happen with every conversation and interaction we have—with colleagues, bosses, and customers and with partners, friends, and family. Without the ability and desire to be straightforward and honest, we cannot create and sustain a caring mindset or achieve a healthy organization, family, or community. Our ability to be straightforward suffers when we become afraid of the consequences, allow our pride and ego to get in the way, or let our perfectionism dominate our thinking.

I have my own perfectionist streak and, during my early years of parenthood, expected my children to emulate my imagined perfection. I expected them to go to college or university and achieve immediate academic success. That didn't happen, at least not on my expected timeline. Eventually I learned that my high expectations and critical feedback during their early years was not balanced nearly enough with positive reinforcing comments and encouraging feedback. Developing this caring mindset has allowed me to better manage my perfectionism without losing the ability to be frank and straightforward. I was delighted, while writing this book, to be able to attend my son's graduation, witness his first major academic success, and appreciate his flourishing career. Conscious leaders are honest, open, frank, and straightforward but also have a caring mindset and convey their message with kindness and compassion.

KINDNESS AND COMPASSION

Speaking candidly requires us to be truthful, straightforward, and unequivocal but not without being kind, compassionate, and caring. Gary Chapman, known for his writing about the five love languages, reminds us that kind words are not always positive words, but when we confront someone for the benefit of the other person in a spirit of meekness, then even confrontation can hold words of kindness; the challenge is to speak the truth and to speak it in love.[102] Chapman suggests listening to ourselves speaking, asking ourselves, *What kind of words do you use?* and replacing unwholesome words with wholesome words, rephrasing negative statements into positive ones. When children come home from school with mediocre grades, rather than a negative comment about another mediocre performance, maybe saying something like, "Although disappointing, that grade can be a stepping-stone to a higher grade next time," before going on to explore the help they need to achieve a higher performance. This is by no means a tolerance of mediocrity but a reframing of the way we speak to show kindness and compassion along with inspiration to improve.

Speaking our truth quietly with respect, courtesy, kindness, and compassion does not have to reduce the impact of speaking candidly. Listening with all the senses, as described earlier in this book, is an essential component of speaking with candor. We have all watched television talk shows on election night where an atmosphere of unrelenting contention and argumentative dialogue results in speakers constantly interrupting each other to the point where hearing individual perspectives becomes impossible. We turn off the television, disgusted with the lack of courtesy shown by the so-called experts. If we begin all our conversations as though the person we are speaking with is one of our closest friends rather than a debate opponent where the only objective is to win the argument, we can create the space for honest and open conversation where we practice both listening with all the senses and speaking candidly.

In an earlier chapter, I referred to meeting Phakyab Rinpoche, a Tibetan lama and the founder and spiritual director of the Vision Healing Buddha Foundation. During his talk, he described compassion and loving kindness as the keys to opening the door to the happiness and inner peace we all seek. Speaking candidly from a place centered around compassion and loving kindness can help enable our messages to be heard clearly by the other person, without any dilution in the strength of our message.

REVEALING OR CONCEALING

Speaking candidly includes the principle and value of full disclosure. Distrust in business and personal relationships is commonplace, and full disclosure is often seen as a risk rather than a benefit. As a leadership coach and management consultant, I cannot even consider withholding certain information as a way to extend the business relationship or increase income because, when that information is ultimately revealed, the client's level of trust will be at risk. Full disclosure means being open and honest at all times in our personal and business relationships, holding nothing back. Jim Dethmer and his colleagues at the Conscious Leadership Group describe three overlapping circles of candor: (1) the circle of truthfulness, where we tell the truth as we see it without lying or distorting the truth; (2) the circle of openness, where we reveal, saying everything we need to say in the spirit of full disclosure, without withholding critical information; and (3) the circle of awareness, where we reveal as much as there is to see without concealing relevant information.[103] Speaking candidly requires *truthfulness*, the accuracy of what I reveal; *openness*, the completeness of my reveal, and *self-awareness* of how accurately and completely I practice full disclosure. Revealing in the spirit of full disclosure helps us authentically connect with people and build trusting relationships. Withholding or concealing inhibits authentic connections and can damage trusting relationships.

BUILDING TRUST THROUGH OUR CONVERSATIONS

Speaking candidly provides a foundation on which to build trust. Fostering trust and truthfulness in all interactions is easier if we come from a place of being harmless. One of the promises made by physicians during their training is "First, do no harm." Although this refers mostly to physical harm, Roger Walsh, researcher and writer, says it also has more subtle implications, such as practicing right speech in order to protect people's feelings or self-esteem.[104] Walsh describes being harmless as a wonderful gift, meaning that we are not acting from, and therefore reinforcing, anger in ourselves so that people are safe in our presence. This allows them to set aside their defenses and pretenses and feel at peace. Reflect for a moment on any recent experiences of causing harm or of feeling harmed. What did you notice about that experience? Being attentive to this principle of doing no harm can help us with the practice of being harmless even when speaking candidly.

Trust in our personal and workplace relationships can be found in most leadership development curriculums. My own learning about trust was enhanced as a result of interactions with Dennis and Michelle Reina, authors of *Trust and Betrayal in the Workplace*.[105] Our capacity for trust begins with building high levels of trust in ourselves, which provides a strong sense of confidence and self-worth. With trust in ourselves, we can develop our capacity for building trust in others, viewing them as increasingly dependable and reliable in fulfilling our expectations. We can earn the trust of others by extending our trust in them. However, trust in our relationships can be fragile, and betrayal of trust—a major intentional betrayal, a minor unintentional betrayal or something in between—can be extremely harmful. The betrayal continuum in Reina's Trust and Betrayal model illustrates examples of intentional betrayal, which ranges from gossiping, backbiting, and accepting credit for another's work to disclosing corporate secrets; unintentional betrayal ranges from failing to honor agreements to delegating responsibility without giving authority. Even minor disputes can escalate into major betrayals if not addressed and resolved.

I recall a situation as a lead consultant for a major change project in the automotive industry where my newly appointed area manager decided to take my place at a critical top team workshop without ever speaking to me about the change in my consulting role. The fact that I was replaced didn't actually cause my feelings of betrayal. Rather, it was the lack of a candid conversation about why the change was appropriate. As it turned out, the decision had nothing to do with my performance and everything to do with the manager's need to be visible at the event. Nevertheless, a betrayal of trust occurred. Reina offers seven steps for healing from betrayal: (1) observe and acknowledge what has happened; (2) allow your feelings to surface; (3) get support; (4) reframe the experience; (5) take responsibility; (6) forgive yourself and others; and (7) let go and move on. Following the seven steps for healing from the betrayal more rigorously may have meant that this example would not come to mind while writing this book, but the memory serves as a valuable reminder of the importance of building trust as well as healing from the betrayal of trust. Often, all it takes is a candid conversation.

CONVERSATIONS THAT MATTER

I have been a participant in and convener of conversations that matter for many years. Consciously creating space for these conversations in large groups, small groups, and intimate settings is an important role for the conscious leader. My involvement in designing and facilitating high-impact events around the world has provided wonderful experiences of effective change and strategy execution processes and real conversations that matter to the future of leaders and organizations.

The nine steps of Craig Neal's Convening Wheel[106] provides a framework for conversations that matter, regardless of the size of the group:

- **At the heart of the matter:** who I am in relationship with others
- **Clarifying intent:** the alignment of our intention with the purpose of our engagement
- **The invitation:** the sincere offering to engage that integrates purpose and intent
- **Setting context:** communicating the form, function, and purpose of our engagement and intent
- **Creating the container:** creating the physical and energetic field within which we meet
- **Hearing all the voices:** each person speaks, is heard, and is present and accounted for
- **Essential conversation:** meaningful exchange within an atmosphere of trust
- **Creation:** something new that emerges from engagements of shared purpose and trust
- **Commitment to action:** an individual or collective agreement to be responsible and accountable for the way forward

Each of the nine steps of the Convening Wheel plays an important part in the process of convening conversations that matter.

Speaking candidly is more often required in small-group and one-to-one situations, and the Convening Wheel can be used in those situations just as well as in larger groups. We have already discussed the importance of giving and receiving feedback as part of learning relentlessly. The added dimension here is in the conscious language we use in these conversations. Conscious language inherent in the principles for speaking candidly include being harmless, clarifying what important words mean, combining advocacy and inquiry, revealing rather than concealing, releasing the need for specific predetermined outcomes, a mindfully slower pace with silence between speakers, and a suspension of judgment.

THE LAST WORD

Before leaving the topic of speaking candidly, I have one additional thought, which is that it really makes a difference what we say and how and when we say it. I recently learned of the death of a good friend, a fellow Toastmaster, and a balloon pilot with whom I had shared the skies on numerous occasions. This friend was apparently fit and healthy, had run numerous marathons and half marathons, and it was on a solitary Saturday afternoon run through the country lanes when he suddenly collapsed and died. He had said goodbye to his wife of many years, expecting to return within the hour, and that was the last time she saw him alive. I don't know the last words they said to each other, but I hope it was something positive and endearing.

Ben Zander, in his 2008 Ted Talk, shares a story about last words and how what we say and how we say it really makes a difference.[107] This was a story of a woman, one of the few survivors from the Auschwitz concentration camp. She went to Auschwitz when she was fifteen years old; her brother was eight, and their parents were lost. She said, "We were in the train going to Auschwitz, and I looked down and saw my brother's shoes were missing. I said, 'Why are you so stupid? Can't you keep your things together for goodness' sake?'" The way an elder sister might speak to a younger brother. Unfortunately, it was the last thing she ever said to him, because she never saw him again. He did not survive. And so, when she came out of Auschwitz, she made a commitment to herself. She said, "I walked out of Auschwitz into life, and I made a vow. And the vow was, 'I will never say anything that couldn't stand as the last thing I ever say to someone.'"

I travel back and forth across the Atlantic frequently, leaving behind immediate family members and close friends for extended periods of time. Despite the frequent video calls, I am always conscious of what I say as I leave, knowing these words may be the last. Living up to a vow to never say anything that couldn't stand as the last thing I ever say to someone may be challenging but is still an important aspiration. If we treat our conversations that matter as if they could be the last thing we will ever say to someone, we will be more conscious of our language and the words we use, whether speaking candidly or simply saying goodbye for now.

ACTING RESPONSIBLY—SPEAKING CANDIDLY

Conscious Leadership Behaviors:

- Speaking clearly and honestly, using language that others can understand
- Clarifying what important words mean
- Being straightforward and unequivocal with a caring mindset
- Speaking truth quietly and confidently, while always being frank and straightforward
- Delivering difficult messages with respect, courtesy, kindness, and compassion
- Fostering trust and truthfulness in all interactions
- Combining advocacy with inquiry
- Revealing in the spirit of full disclosure rather than concealing information
- Creating spaces for conversations that matter
- Saying nothing that couldn't stand as the last thing we ever say to someone

CHAPTER 8

Acting with Integrity

In simple terms, acting with integrity is doing what you say you will do, backing up words with actions, and practicing what you believe is right. Beyond that, in the context of conscious leadership, acting with integrity means aligning actions with values, purpose, intentions, and commitments, knowing who you are and how you show up, being impeccable with your word, and acting ethically for the good of all. Integrity is about taking a stand, standing up for what is right, mastering ego, and treating everyone with respect. Integrity is also about leading from the inside out with authenticity, transparency, vulnerability, humility, and stewardship. Acting with integrity is the antithesis of workplace bullying, also included in this chapter.

Acting with integrity is closely aligned to character and presence, which was discussed in the chapter on living mindfully. Character can be thought about as who we are; presence is about how we show up. Acting with integrity requires us to be conscious of our character and presence as well as all the conscious leadership practices described in the chapters of this book.

DOING WHAT YOU SAY YOU WILL DO

A foundation for acting with integrity is the basic principle of doing what you say you will do. An even stronger principle is the first of the four agreements offered by Don Miguel Ruiz, a Mexican author of Toltec spiritualist texts: be impeccable with your word.[108] Considering the word as a force, a powerful tool through which our dreams, thoughts, intentions, and commitments are manifested, we are reminded of the importance of the words we use when speaking and writing. Words can both create and destroy, engage and disconnect, inspire and discourage. Impeccability, although having a Christian connotation of being without sin, may also be considered as flawless, faultless, or perfect. When you are impeccable, you take responsibility for your actions, which is the theme of this series of practices. Conscious leaders are aware of the words they use when speaking and writing, live to the highest ethical standards, and are impeccable with their word; they honor their commitments, keep their promises, and stand up for what is right.

TAKING A STAND

Someone once said that if you don't stand for something, you'll *do* just about anything, or put another way, you either stand for something or fall for anything. Standing up for what is right, for what we believe in, provides a center within us from which to practice integrity. Global visionary Lynn Twist, founder of the Soul of Money Institute, puts it this way: "Taking a stand is a way of living and being that draws on a place within yourself that is at the very heart of where you are. When you take a stand, it gives you authenticity, power, and clarity. You find your place in the universe, and you have the capacity to move the world."[109] Conscious leaders stand up for what is right, for what they believe in. They stand for something, and they know what they stand for. This is not simply about following a set of principles. To really stand for something, we must make tough choices; it is about who we are and how we show up, about what we will *not* do as much as what we *will* do, and about being the best *for* the world rather than the best *in* the world.

Aligning with the truth-telling described in the previous chapter about speaking candidly, Gary Chapman, author of *Love as a Way of Life*, offers examples of standing on the side of truth.[110] When William Wilberforce took his first public stand against human slavery in England in 1789, he was taking the side of truth and justice even though it was a very unpopular stance, but because of his effort in the face of opposition, that dark chapter in history was closed, and the British slave trade was declared illegal in 1807. More than a century later, in 1955, civil rights activist Rosa Parks's refusal to surrender her seat to a white passenger on a public bus in

Montgomery, Alabama, spurred on a citywide boycott and helped launch nationwide efforts to end segregation of public facilities. She didn't set out to become the first lady of civil rights, but by taking a stand, in fact *refusing* to stand and give up her seat, she was standing for what she believed in. Rosa Parks said, "I would like to be known as a person who is concerned about freedom and equality and justice and prosperity for all people." By taking a stand, Rosa Parks's act of defiance had a far-reaching impact and inspired many others to stand up with her.

This raises the question for each of us to consider: what do I stand for? We all need a moral compass that serves as a guide to our decisions based on our morals and virtues, our values and principles, our purpose and intentions, and what is good for others more than ourselves. We need to stand up for what we believe is right. Much of what I stand for will be evident in the contents of this book, but as a local example, living part-time on South Florida's Atlantic coast, environmental issues relating to rising sea levels, plastic pollution of the oceans, water conservation, and plans to send massive amounts of polluted lake water south to the Everglades National Park are important. Polluted lake water is a complex issue with multiple stakeholders. I will stand up to ensure government officials take the right action to address the damaging discharges from the lake to the estuaries by building long-promised reservoirs but will not accept solutions that negatively affect the livelihoods of local farmers and their hardworking farmworkers.

We all fail to honor our own values and sense of purpose sometimes, but instead of making excuses, let us ask this question: "When I fail, do I commit to being better and doing better next time?" Get to the place where, in the words often attributed to Ralph Waldo Emerson, "What you do speaks so loudly that I cannot hear what you say." Conscious leaders stand up for what they believe in, act on their beliefs, engage in society, and take a public stand for what matters most. What matters to you? What do you stand for? What would you never compromise? If you don't stand for something, you'll do just about anything. It is time to stand up for what is right. Consider these questions: What are you doing here on this planet? What is your purpose? What do you hold as important—what are your values? What are you committed to seeing happen? How well are your intentions aligned with your vision of the future?

Taking a stand may be related to major issues such as global warming and the future of our planet, the increasing divide between the rich and poor, toxic working environments, or on the behaviors of people in our immediate environment. There are many causes to support and issues where we can take a stand, but I invite you to consider Howard Thurman's advice: "Do not ask yourself what the world needs. Ask yourself what makes you come alive and do that. Because what the world needs is people who have come alive." Live your life doing what you really believe is the right thing to do, where you are personally prepared to take a stand. Do not adopt a generic stance taken by the masses or the safe route that will not be challenged. Choose something on which you are prepared to take responsible action every day.

LEADING FROM THE INSIDE OUT

We have already noted the importance of leading from the inside out in the chapter on living mindfully, but let's explore some of the deeper characteristics of conscious leaders who act with integrity: authenticity, transparency, vulnerability, humility, and stewardship. Definitions of these characteristics overlap, but each brings a unique perspective for the aspiring conscious leader.

AUTHENTICITY

Being authentic means being real or genuine, not copied or false. To be authentic, you must wake up and notice what is going on inside and outside. You have to know who you are, why you are here, what your purpose is, what your commitments are, and what you stand for. Kevin Cashman, author of *Leadership from the Inside Out*, defines authenticity as the continual process of building self-awareness of our whole person, being transparent with others about our strengths and limitations, and, more than just walking the talk, authenticity means embodying your talk at a very deep level.[111]

If we were considering buying a Picasso original or a thoroughbred racehorse, we would likely consider it worthwhile to determine the authenticity of the painting or the lineage of the horse. Michael Carroll suggests that in Buddhism, our search for human authenticity is also a practical and worthy matter in which we experience directly the original authority from which we arise, and he suggests that to be authentic is to stop imitating who we would like to be and acknowledge who we are already; that being authentic is the fundamental proclamation that *who we are* and *where we are* arises from our original authority, one that makes us decent, intelligent, and profoundly resourceful.[112]

Conscious leadership is not the same as authentic leadership. Conscious leaders are likely to be authentic leaders, but authentic leaders may not be conscious leaders. Gina Hayden, cofounder of the Global Center for Conscious Leadership, suggests that the key difference is about our ability to transform ourselves. The inner journey to conscious leadership is a transformational one; being authentic is an essential characteristic of how we show up on that journey. Hayden refers to being authentic as like the sun shining through from behind the clouds we use as cover-up and protection; the more we remove these clouds, the more our essential authenticity can shine through and be experienced by others.[113] Our authentic self already exists and is revealed in our character and presence, as we have explored in the chapter on living mindfully.

TRANSPARENCY

Transparency is closely related to authenticity, openness, and trust, and in the wake of recent irresponsible and often unethical behaviors of leaders in business and government, people are demanding ethical cultures where transparency is highly valued. Transparency is the new leadership imperative. In discussing radical transparency, Chris Laszlo and his fellow researchers suggested that, fueled by unprecedented activism in the civil sector and supported by rapid developments in information technology, transparency has become an unavoidable aspect of modern corporate life.[114] Any interested person or group can now peer into an organization and find and publicize impacts on society and nature that used to be hidden from public scrutiny.

In the United States, the Sarbanes-Oxley Act, designed to protect investors by improving the accuracy and reliability of corporate disclosures, has helped because business leaders now are required to operate by a set of rules; however, transparency doesn't mean there are no secrets. Leaders must navigate a fine line between transparency with multiple stakeholders and protection of sensitive information. Mark Moreland, president of Full Sail Brewing, believes transparency is critical to organizational success, saying, "If you do not have leaders who are living up to their stated expectations around transparency, then you do not have the right leaders. Leaders need to be actively engaged in and driving this conversation, helping coach, guide, and amplify the organization's transparency."[115]

Bob Johansen, a distinguished fellow at the Institute for the Future and author of *Leaders Make the Future*, describes quiet transparency as an ability to be open and authentic about what matters, without being overly self-promoting.[116] This begins with being quiet, creating calm, and listening for the future. In that future, leaders are more likely to be open about almost everything, unless there is a need to conceal, and in today's world of instantaneous multimedia, concealment may not be easy. Conscious leaders have a heightened awareness of their levels of transparency, but according to Johansen, leaders may not get to decide what transparency means and how it is measured. The degree of transparency expected of organizational leaders will be established by the multiple stakeholders of the organization. Conscious leaders will be aware of these expectations, aspiring to live up to them without being self-promotional about their transparency. Quiet transparency also includes vulnerability and humility.

VULNERABILITY

Being vulnerable is described in the *Oxford English Dictionary* as being exposed to the possibility of being attacked or harmed, either physically or emotionally. Vulnerability in leaders is the degree to which we allow ourselves to be exposed to the risk of harm. There is both risk and power in being vulnerable. The power in vulnerability is described in the Center for Creative Leadership Handbook of Leadership Development: "Personal vulnerability opens the door to being genuine, human, and authentic with others, but the truth is that most leaders wear protective masks that they do not remove easily or lightly. It is as if they have been taught to hide or disguise any signs of fear, frustration, or personal gain lest it leak out and somehow undermine their credibility as a leader of others."[117] The challenge for the conscious leader is in removing the mask and showing up with confidence, awareness, and genuine authenticity.

I am grateful for Brené Brown's research and her writings on how the courage to be vulnerable transforms the way we live, love, parent, and lead.[118] Defining vulnerability as uncertainty, risk, and emotional exposure, Brown identifies vulnerability myths, including: (1) vulnerability is weakness; (2) I don't do vulnerability; (3) vulnerability is letting it all hang out; (4) we can go it alone. After debunking these myths, Brown suggests that "vulnerability is the birthplace of love, belonging, joy, courage, empathy, and creativity. It is the source of hope, empathy, accountability, and authenticity." If we want greater clarity in our purpose or deeper, more meaningful spiritual lives, vulnerability is the path.

Another perspective on vulnerability comes from Michael Carroll, author of *The Mindful Leader*, who explains that the Tibetan word for vulnerable openness is *Jinpa*, which means "complete generosity."[119] This generosity may require the dropping of our own point of view, to lead from a place of being open to vulnerability, creating the space for others to share their points of view even at the risk of having to let go of long-held positions on certain issues. Such vulnerability can be freeing because we stop wrestling with our personal anxieties and simply expose ourselves to the world around us, overcoming fearful and unfamiliar emotions and creating opportunities to genuinely lead and inspire others. Conscious leaders strive to overcome the fears associated with personal vulnerability and, using a baseball analogy, continue to step up to the plate, ready to hit despite a series of previous strikeouts.

HUMILITY

The concept of humility in leaders is not new. More than fifty years ago, Robert Greenleaf, the founder of the modern servant leadership movement, suggested that servant leadership begins with the natural feeling of wanting to serve, to serve first, and this conscious desire to serve brings with it the aspiration to lead.[120] More recently, Jim Collins, writing about a Level 5 Leadership in the book *Good to Great*, reported, "We were surprised, shocked really, to discover the type of leadership required for turning a good company into a great one. Compared to high profile leaders with big personalities who make headlines and become celebrities, the good-to-great leaders seem to have come from Mars. Self-effacing, quiet, reserved, even shy—these leaders are a paradoxical blend of personal humility and professional will."[121] We may sometimes think of humility as a weak character trait, but humility affirms the worth of someone else and creates the space for others to step up. This can be a source of great joy for the conscious leader.

I spent a week with culture guru Edgar Schein at the Cape Cod Institute many years ago learning from the master about organizational culture. In his recent book, Schein describes humble inquiry as the fine art of drawing someone out, asking questions to which you do not already know the answer, and building a relationship on curiosity and interest in the other person.[122] Being humble requires us to be in the present moment, cultivating a quiet and profound appreciation of the contributions of others. Humble leaders are inclusive, curious, open to the perspectives of others, caring, and they serve first and then lead. While still striving to align responsible actions with goals and intentions, conscious leaders show up with exceptional humility.

STEWARDSHIP

Being a good steward means taking responsible action in service of people and resources within our sphere of influence. Like many of the attributes of conscious leaders, stewardship means putting people first, not using them for our own ends but serving them and being a good steward of their lives. It is about choosing service over self-interest.

Peter Block, author of *Stewardship: Choosing Service Over Self Interest*, who I first met in New York about twenty years ago, wrote, "Stewardship is to hold something in trust for another; a choice to act in service of the long run and a choice to act in the service of those with little power."[123] Although recognizing that the idea of stewardship is somewhat elusive and suffers from ambiguity, the practice of stewardship still provides a framework for thriving in the complexity of this modern age. Ultimately, we must make a choice between service and self-interest. We exist in an age of entitlement and egocentricity. But can we come from a place of service?

Can we ask, "How may I help you?" "How may I serve this person or this organization?"

Stewardship can also be applied to purpose, which aligns with the earlier chapter on exploring purposefully. Acting responsibly with integrity requires us to be stewards of our individual purpose as well as our organizational purpose. Roy Spence describes six principles for being stewards of purpose: (1) be the torch bearer of purpose; (2) believe in purpose before profits; (3) use purpose to create alignment and drive performance; (4) keep in mind what you are fighting for; (5) use purpose, not just personality, to lead; and (6) do right by your purpose.[124] Being good stewards of our purpose, people, and the planet is a requirement for acting responsibly and with integrity.

MASTERING EGO

Ego often gets a bad rap, yet as something that provides a sense of who we really are, understanding and mastering our ego is an essential part of acting with integrity. This is not so much about leaving our ego at the door; rather it is about bringing it with us to use as a lens through which to look at how we behave. As conscious leaders, understanding our ego begins with the practice of noticing what is going on, becoming increasingly self-aware, and setting personal intentions about how we wish to show up in the world. As Jim Collins noted in *Good to Great*, it is not that Level 5 leaders have no ego or self-interest but that they channel their ego needs away from themselves and into the larger goal of building a great company.[125]

Ego is defined in the *Oxford English Dictionary* as a person's sense of self-esteem or self-importance. These two aspects of our ego may be considered as healthy and unhealthy egos, a distinction that Rosalie Chamberlain, author of *Conscious Leadership in the Workplace*, suggests is a sense of self that serves us compared to one that does not.[126] The unhealthy ego, focused on our own self-importance, is often driven by fear and contains the negativity, unhealthy competition, and victimhood of the drama triangle. Showing up with our unhealthy ego, we may notice how we compare ourselves to others, wanting to be better than them, and behaving in a way that is self-promoting rather than being of service to others and serving the greater good. I have often seen this in leaders who in meetings present their ideas and solutions first, often in a way that inhibits contributions from others, and then always want the last word in any discussion as well.

Unhealthy ego may show up as what Gina Hayden[127] refers to as "symptoms of separation" that conscious leaders can be on the lookout for. These unhealthy ego-based symptoms may present themselves as playing it safe, withholding contributions for fear of reprisal or not fitting in or to subtly punish or control; being right, being attached to a position, justifying and defending positions, and unwilling to consider alternatives; looking good, posturing or self-promoting to demonstrate personal importance; or playing the victim, blaming others rather than taking responsibility for the situation. Conscious leaders are aware of an unwanted appearance of the unhealthy ego.

A strong sense of self-esteem allows us to call on our higher self, to show up with confidence and a belief that solutions will emerge from meaningful conversations with engaged individuals, not necessarily from us as the self-professed expert in the field. In idea generation and problem-solving situations, I have observed that it is often the quiet, reluctant member of a group who has the best ideas. Conscious leaders with a healthy ego seek to create spaces where it is possible to hear all the voices, combining advocacy with inquiry, and being open to new innovative possibilities we may never have imagined. The ego is a tool we can use to navigate the world. When we notice what is going on around and within us and are in touch with our purpose and higher self, our awareness and mastery of our healthy and unhealthy egos can help us show up authentically and act with integrity.

WORKPLACE BULLYING

Bullying in the workplace may at first appear a surprising topic for this section of the book, but aspiring conscious leaders acting with integrity must stand up against workplace bullying. While preparing to write this book, I sat down with Andrew Faas, author of *From Bully to Bull's-Eye*,[128] to talk among other things about his partnering with Mental Health America in an initiative to promote psychologically healthy, safe, and fair workplaces. I was serving as the chair of the board of directors of the Mental Health Association of Palm Beach County and supporting a local conscious business initiative focusing on mental well-being in the workplace. Insights gained during this conversation convinced me that this was an important topic for the aspiring conscious leader to better understand.

The choice of working for a conscious leader or a workplace bully appears at first sight to be a no-brainer. Who would choose to work for a workplace bully? Yet, according to Faas, bullying in the workplace is one of the biggest societal and economic issues we face. Supporting this observation, findings from doctoral research conducted by Dr. Judy Blando, an expert on workplace bullying, showed that nearly 75 percent of employees had witnessed mistreatment of coworkers sometime throughout their careers, and 27 percent admitted to being a target of a workplace bully in the previous twelve months.[129] In 74 percent of the cases explored by Faas, the bullying was from boss to subordinate. In these cases, the bullied are often unable to take action due to fear of losing their job. Many are actively looking for another job. You may dismiss these claims of workplace bullying as a case of victimhood. Many of us take on the role of victim, blaming and complaining about how things happen to us. The conscious leader recognizes people caught in the victim trap where they feel powerless to change. Rather than take the role of rescuer or the hero in the drama triangle, conscious leaders take on the role of coach to help the victim take responsibility for their life.

In this book, I have generally focused on the positive behaviors of aspiring conscious leaders rather than pointing to the more negative behaviors of the autocratic, dictatorial, or narcissistic leader often representative of the workplace bully. Although it is unlikely that you are a workplace bully, you may be noticing bullying behaviors in your organization. If you have a culture of workplace bullying, it is likely that you already have high employee turnover, and more than half of your employees may be actively job hunting. A culture of bullying can create a highly toxic workplace where employees become disengaged and unproductive, resulting in significant declines in workplace performance. Acting with integrity requires the aspiring conscious leader to confront the workplace bully and change toxic workplaces into positive cultures where people come to work because they want to, not because they have to.

Numerous examples of workplace bullying are included in Faas's book, *From Bully to Bull's-Eye*, some of which, at first sight, you might see as commonplace; still, they represent stressful workplace situations unacceptable to the aspiring conscious leader. I am grateful to author Andrew Faas for his permission to include one such story from his book. This is Vera's story, from victim to villain.

Vera, a marketing manager for an appliance manufacturer for nine years, was given the option to resign or be fired from her position. The reasons given for her termination were poor performance and insubordination. Not wanting to jeopardize her ability to relocate, she agreed to resign and received a modest severance.

Vera's last formal performance review was just over a year before, when she received an "exceeds expectations" rating. She also received an above-average merit increase and an incentive payout recognizing that she met all of her individual performance objectives. Over the previous eight years, Vera was rated and viewed as a high performer.

Six months after that last performance review, as part of a restructuring, Vera's reporting relationship changed, and Mark, who was also a marketing manager, became the director of the department and Vera's boss. Vera felt that she was more qualified than Mark but recognized that he had more of a presence, which, in the culture of the organization, counted for more. While Vera was disappointed that she was not promoted, she indicated to Mark that she would support him.

When they were peers, Mark viewed Vera as a threat. He would upstage her when the opportunity presented itself, and he often took credit for work she did. Vera's former boss recognized this and told her not to worry about it, that this was part of Mark's aggressive nature; she would get credit for her contributions. Over the years, Vera and Mark were equally exposed to senior executives to review marketing plans and major initiatives. Usually, Vera did most of the preparation work, and Mark made the presentation. Vera was okay with this, as she was not comfortable with public speaking. During the discussion periods, however, it was apparent that Vera was better prepared than Mark, manifesting a classic case of style over substance.

When Mark became the director, he started excluding Vera from the monthly marketing review meetings with senior management. Vera continued to prepare the presentations, and her only feedback came when Mark could not answer a question, naming Vera for not having prepped him well enough. In subsequent meetings, Vera added yet more notes for Mark to reference, anticipating the questions he would be asked. Mark continued to struggle during the discussion periods. When the CEO suggested publicly that Vera should attend the meetings, Mark was concerned about her showing him up and jeopardizing his position. Mark resolved to get rid of Vera.

Mark met with his boss and Tim, the head of human resources, to voice his dissatisfaction with Vera's work and to state that he wanted to let her go. They challenged Mark based on Vera's favorable performance reviews and the previous director's high opinion of her. Mark countered that the previous director covered up Vera's deficiencies, that he (Mark) carried most of the weight, and Vera resented his promotion. He also insinuated that she and the previous director had more than a professional relationship. The head of human resources told Mark that to fire Vera, he had to build a case.

So, he did. He kept important information from her, excluded her from meetings, gave her unrealistic targets and timelines, and constantly badgered her. This affected her performance and her attitude. When she challenged Mark, he reprimanded her citing insubordination, sending copies to the vice president and Tim. Each time a mistake was made, a target or timeline not reached, Vera received a written warning, again, with copies to the vice president and Tim. In addition to the written warnings, Vera was subjected to verbal abuse, threats, and intimidation.

Knowing Mark as she did, it occurred to Vera that she was being set up. Because Mark could prove that her performance was deteriorating, she started to blame herself for the position she was in. This made her increasingly irritable, causing more confrontations with Mark, giving Mark even more ammunition. Others in the department observed some of what was going on, and most had their own challenges with Mark. Vera previously had a good working relationship with them; most sought her help, which she readily gave. When it became apparent that she was targeted, the department shunned her, and she became the subject of a lot of water cooler chats. Mark fed the gossip mill by telling people how poorly Vera was handling the situation and that she "did not have her boyfriend there to protect her."

Because of her frustration with the situation and herself, she started lashing out at others in the department. This strained relationships and was a factor in no one coming to her defense. They rationalized that Vera was not handling the situation well. Mark sent some of them to Tim to complain about Vera. Some only went because they were afraid not to, while others happily complied.

Vera's doctor strongly recommended that she go on disability for stress. But Tim told her the company wouldn't pay disability benefits, as they didn't consider stress a disability. He further told her that it would be viewed as avoiding disciplinary action for her performance and attitude, and her action would be without cause, which would result in termination. Vera decided not to go on disability. Not knowing what to do next, Vera complained to Tim that Mark was bullying her and setting her up to be fired. Tim defended Mark's actions and behaviors, suggesting that the issue was Vera's performance and attitude and, unless there was a significant improvement, the company would have no choice but to terminate her. Tim suggested that they meet with Mark to discuss it. Vera was not comfortable with this but felt she had no choice.

At the meeting, Tim told Mark that Vera had lodged a complaint about being bullied. Mark told Vera and Tim that he was not bullying but only doing his job, correcting deficiencies, and reacting when he felt that Vera was not being respectful. He went on to say that he was sorry that Vera felt the way she did, that he meant no harm. Tim suggested that this was more of a personality clash and Mark's style may be a bit aggressive. Mark agreed with this assessment and promised to work on his communication with Vera, adding, "I understand you are still quite upset with not getting the promotion, but for this to work, you have to get over it."

After the meeting, Mark followed her into her office, closed the door, and said, "Now you have really gone too [expletive] far! How dare you accuse me of bullying? You're the one who started all of this. You have never been any good, and you never will be. Why don't you do everyone a favor and quit?" Vera burst into tears and slapped Mark across the face. Mark picked up the phone, called Tim, and said, "I want you to fire that bitch right now. She just hit me." Without getting Vera's side of the story, Tim gave Vera the option to be fired or resign.

The bullying did not stop there. An advertising agency with whom the company had a long-standing relationship thought highly of Vera and offered to hire her with the understanding that she would not be assigned any work related to her previous employer. When Mark learned of their intent, he told the agency CEO, "If you hire her, you will lose this account." Vera was not hired and continued looking for employment. She was blacklisted, and because it's a small world, it was almost impossible for her to gain comparable employment in her field.

It is easy to see how the drama triangle played out in this situation, and it may be easy to blame Vera for becoming the victim in this case. The behavior of Vera's new boss, the human resources manager, and her colleagues play out in organizations every day. For the aspiring conscious leader, the behavior of each of the players is unacceptable. Awareness of any of these behaviors in ourselves is the first step in enabling us to behave more mindfully. Awareness of these behaviors in others is sometimes easier but no less important. The opportunity is in noticing these behaviors, setting intention around how we are going to show up in those situations, and acting with integrity to confront the actors wherever they may be. It is time to be awake at work and step beyond the silence of fear.

Whether you are the bully, one of the bullied, a bystander, or a concerned friend, conscious leadership practices can help. Notice what is going on in your workplace or in your working relationships. Set a clear intention to prevent the consequences of workplace bullying for you, your coworkers, and the leaders in your organization. Take responsibility for yourself and act responsibly in your interactions with others in your workplace. Is your workplace psychologically safe? Ask yourself, "What am I doing about workplace bullying?"

WHEN NO ONE IS LOOKING

We can all practice acting with integrity when we are being observed, but our true character is reflected in what we do when no one is looking. My apartment in Florida overlooks the beach. I often sit on the balcony to read or practice mindfulness meditation. The beach is generally quiet with a few people lying out in the sun and others walking alone or in small groups, some with their dogs. Most dog owners carry the requisite plastic bag to pick up after the dog. One day as I was looking out over the beach, I saw a dog leaving a deposit on the sand. The dog's owner looked around to see if anyone was watching, kicked sand over the poop, and walked away. Who knows who stepped on that piece of sand. The owner was not acting with integrity. He also didn't realize how many people may have been watching from the apartments overlooking the beach.

Automotive manufacturers have had their fair share of scandals that reflect a lack of integrity. Volkswagen installed emissions software on more than ten million of their diesel cars sold worldwide that allowed them to dupe environmental emissions testing agencies into thinking the vehicles were in compliance by switching between two distinct operating modes. Compliance demonstrated during testing under one operating mode was not achieved during normal driving conditions where computer software switched to another operating mode. This likely delivered higher power and lower fuel consumption but also permitted heavier nitrogen-oxide emissions, a smog-forming pollutant linked to lung cancer. Apparently, the cheating devices had been installed in Volkswagen vehicles for years. Leaders of the Volkswagen organization have paid the price, losing their jobs, fixing vehicles in the field, and paying compensation and penalties, but the long-term loss of reputation is impossible to calculate. The extent to which organizational leaders were aware of this unethical behavior remains unclear, but developing a culture of acting with integrity is now likely to be a high priority.

Bill Hybels, in his book, *Who You Are When No One's Looking,* has pointed the way to acting with integrity for more than thirty years.[130] Hybels recommends choosing consistency, resisting a compromise, insisting on truth in relationships, and breaking the hostility cycle. If a tree falls in a forest and no one is around to hear it, does it make a sound? What we do when no one is watching is a true test of the degree to which we are acting with integrity, of our character and presence, and being true to ourselves.

As we have seen in this chapter, acting with integrity is an all-encompassing topic beyond simply doing what you say you will do. It is about backing up your words with actions and taking a stand; leading from the inside out with authenticity, transparency, vulnerability, humility, and stewardship. It is about mastering ego and eliminating workplace bullying. It is about acting with integrity always, even when no one is looking.

ACTING RESPONSIBLY—ACTING WITH INTEGRITY

Conscious Leadership Behaviors:

- Doing what we say we will do, backing up our words with actions
- Being impeccable with our word
- Meeting commitments
- Treating others with dignity and respect
- Standing up for what is right
- Leading with authenticity, transparency, vulnerability, and humility
- Being a good steward for purpose, people, and the planet
- Mastering ego with awareness and understanding
- Eliminating toxicity in the workplace
- Acting with integrity even when no one is looking

CHAPTER 9

Taking Responsible Action

Conscious leaders take responsibility for their impact on the world. Taking responsible action means different things to different people and could be considered along a continuum of impact. You may be committed to great causes such as planetary sustainability or world peace; you may have a profound sense of responsibility for the lives entrusted to you at work or at home; you may be passionate about local initiatives relating to criminal justice, domestic violence, poverty, or homelessness; or you may be committed to changing the way you show up and behave at home or in the workplace. Taking responsible action means acting responsibly always, being socially and environmentally responsible, taking full responsibility for all aspects of our lives, and actively supporting others aspiring to take responsible action. Conscious leaders take personal responsibility for their impact on the world and support collective responsibility, leading with energy and inspiration, and making a difference.

I first heard the star thrower story from Joel Barker,[131] and although well known, it is worth sharing here. The story, inspired by the writing of scientist and poet Loren Eiseley, is of a wise man, much like Eiseley himself, who used to go to the ocean to do his writing. The wise man had a habit of walking on the beach before he began his work. One day he was walking along the shore. As he looked down the beach, he saw a human figure moving like a dancer. He smiled to himself to think of someone who would dance to the day. He began to walk faster to catch up. As he got closer, he saw that it was a young man, and the young man wasn't dancing, but instead he was reaching down to the shore, picking something up, and very gently throwing it into the ocean. As he got closer, he called out, "Good morning! What are you doing?" The young man paused, looked up, and replied, "Throwing starfish into the ocean." He asked, "Why are you throwing starfish into the ocean?" to which the young man replied, "The sun is up, and the tide is going out. And if I don't throw them in, they'll die." "But young man, don't you realize that there are miles and miles of beach and starfish all along it? You can't possibly make a difference!" The young man listened politely. Then he bent down, picked up another starfish, and threw it into the sea, past the breaking waves. "It made a difference for that one!"

The Florida beach I walk along doesn't have starfish, but it does have turtles. Mother turtles show up during the night, dig sand pits, lay their eggs, cover up the nest, and, leaving their distinctive turtle tracks in the sand, head back to the ocean only to return to the same stretch of beach the following year. After six weeks or so, turtle hatchlings can be seen battling their way from the nest across the sand and the uneven reef to reach the ocean before being picked off by predatory birds. As I see them battling across the rocks, I think of the starfish and want to help them on their way to the ocean, but in the case of the turtle hatchlings, the responsible action is to let them make their own way there, during which time they will build up the muscles in their flippers that will allow them to swim the many thousands of miles across the oceans. Taking responsible action can take many forms; choosing can be difficult.

Choosing between right and wrong is something most of us learned during our early years, but many times we are required to choose between right and right. This is not just about ethical choices but day-to-day decisions that are part of a leader's genuine responsibilities to choose the best path forward even when there are multiple right answers. Conscious leaders take personal responsibility for their own actions as well as recognizing and mentoring others who are taking personal responsibility.

PERSONAL RESPONSIBILITY

Taking the position that, as an aspiring conscious leader, "I am responsible at all times, in all places, under all circumstances, without exception"[132] could be considered sufficient for this section on personal responsibility, but let's explore specific behaviors that exhibit personal responsibility. More than simply doing what is right because it's the right thing to do, taking personal responsibility for everything we say and do is about recognizing the impact we have on people and things around us. Conscious leaders believe that the right actions undertaken for the right reasons generally lead to good outcomes over time.

Having *taking responsible action* as the last of the individual conscious leadership practices described in this book was a conscious decision. Taking personal responsibility for our actions requires us to be aware of the first eight practices in the book. Being awake and noticing what is going on around us is a prerequisite to being personally responsible and making responsible decisions. Making choices and decisions that reflect our personal responsibility requires clarity of purpose, a possibility mindset, and personal commitment to action aligned with our intentions.

As aspiring conscious leaders, we all crave a world filled with love and care. Yet we live in a world where we are taught to look out for ourselves, maximize financial performance in our business and private lives, and do what we need to do to get ahead, even at the expense of the people we care about. Taking personal responsibility for ourselves is important but not at the expense of others. Although experiencing a loving and caring world beyond our immediate family often feels unattainable, we are responsible for believing in what is possible. We have a personal responsibility to strive for deep connection, care, and love in our relationships in our private and business lives.

Most of us are familiar with the words of a Robert Frost poem: "Two roads diverged in a wood, and I—I took the one less traveled by, and that has made all the difference." A few years ago, as part of a research study into purposeful aging, I interviewed Phoebe Ballard, coauthor of the book *Turning Points*.[133] Some of our personal turning points are outside of our control, but as Ballard pointed out, all of us must embrace the idea that we are the only ones in control of our working lives. Turning points in our careers are easily recognized. The decision to accept a new job offer, either within the same organization or with a new company, represents a major milestone. Strategic decisions about future direction can also be quite memorable. What may be less memorable are how we respond and the decisions we take during our daily interactions with others. Turning points in our relationships with others during these daily interactions arise frequently, and we have a personal responsibility to notice what is going on and to act responsibility for the good of the relationship.

How we respond in different situations may depend on external factors and circumstances or our inner instincts. In any case, we always have a choice in how we respond. The hand we are dealt in a game of cards is not within our control, but we can do our best with the cards we have. You may not be responsible for the situation you find yourself in, but you are responsible for what you do in that situation. You are not responsible for the poverty in the world; you didn't start it, and you didn't worsen it, but you are able to respond to it in any way you choose. You may not be responsible for the toxic workplace you find yourself in, but how you respond to that situation is your personal responsibility. How we respond in each situation is always up to us.

Personal responsibility requires that we keep trying regardless of the obstacles that come up. My mother always used to say, "If at first you don't succeed, try, try, and try again." It is often easier to quit trying than to endure. It may have been easier to quit writing this book than to endure the daily commitment to writing and editing. It may be easier to walk away from an argument at work than to stay and work through the conflict. It may be easier to accept a problematic relationship than to endure the consequences of making the break, walking away, and beginning the process of building a new one. It may be easier to tell others how to act rather than collaborating to build consensus around change. It may be easier to recede into the background than to take a stand and inspire action about something we care deeply about. We build leadership strengths by enduring, by crashing through the quitting points. This is our personal responsibility.

Taking personal responsibility for our actions requires conscious decision-making. Decisions that affect us only are quite different from the decisions that affect others. As I thought more about personal responsibility, I found myself resonating with Michael Carroll's single guiding principle: "More often than not, seeking success for ourselves proves pointless and shallow, whereas seeking success and inspiration for others almost always delivers prosperity and well-being right into our hands."[134] Although personal responsibility requires us to look inward first, personal fulfillment never comes through self-gratification.

COLLECTIVE RESPONSIBILITY

Everyone is important and worthy of care, and Bob Chapman, coauthor of *Everybody Matters*, suggests we start operating from the deepest sense of what is right, acting with a profound sense of responsibility for the lives entrusted to us.[135] This philosophy provides a bridge between our personal responsibilities for actions directly impacting us to taking responsible actions that impact the people around us and the world at large. Responsibility for people shows up in the practices of speaking candidly and acting with integrity. A genuine caring for people in our families, our social circles, our workplaces, and around the world enables us to practice taking collective responsibility.

This sense of responsibility can also be a trap. Joseph Jaworski, founder of the American Leadership Forum, reminds us to avoid the traps of responsibility, dependency, and overactivity, while sharing his experience of feeling responsible for all the people involved in his organization, of feeling indispensable to the whole process, and thinking everyone was depending on him.[136] Distinguishing between acting with a profound sense responsibility for the lives of people entrusted to us and being obsessively worried about their dependence on us will help us avoid the trap of overactivity and taking on too much.

While writing this book, I was serving as president of the board of trustees for a liberal religious congregation. With a minister in place, this role was challenging but not onerous. However, the minister left, and we endured a long period without one, increasing exponentially my sense of responsibility for the nearly two hundred members and friends in the congregation. This was an opportunity to practice conscious leadership. Starting with an intention of serving first, the practices described in this book, along with the associated behaviors, provided a guide for this leadership role. The board of trustees had difficult decisions to make on behalf of the congregation. Many decisions, taken after extensive consultation and conversation, were never likely to please everybody. Reducing the hours of the administrative assistant was one of those decisions. A reduction in hours would help us be fiscally responsible with the financial contributions of the congregation, but the resulting loss of income for the administrator may bring financial hardship for her.

Summer hours had been discussed in previous years, but no action had ever been taken. Members felt responsible for the well-being of the long-serving administrator. The approved budget was tight, and as president of the board of trustees, I had made a commitment to continue to seek ways to reduce expenses wherever possible. The right choice was to reduce the administrator's hours. Another right choice, as a caring leader acting with a profound sense of responsibility for the administrator's well-being, was not to reduce those hours. Taking responsible action in these cases, choosing between right and right, is never easy. As a conscious leader, noticing what is going on around us, hearing all the voices, and setting a clear intention to serve, may not make the decision easier but helps to live with the decisions made based on strong beliefs as a foundation for taking responsible action. Curiously, in this case, the board president only has a vote when the voting of other members of the board results in a tie, which was not the case here. Nevertheless, the leader's influence can be significant and the responsibility no less. Although there is a collective responsibility among board members, personal responsibility is at the heart of the matter and influences collective responsibility.

As can be seen from this situation, there are two sides to collective responsibility. Democratic decision-making means taking responsible action as a group where decisions and choices may be far from unanimous. Another aspect of collective responsibility is the duty we feel toward the greater whole of which we are all part. *The Weight of a Snowflake* is a classic story with numerous variations. Here is a simple version of the snowflake story:

> *"Tell me the weight of a snowflake," a sparrow asked a wild dove. "Nothing more than nothing" was the answer. "In that case, I must tell a marvelous story," said the sparrow. "I was sitting on a branch of a fir tree, close to its trunk, when it began to snow, not heavily, not a giant blizzard, no, just like in a dream, without any violence. Since I didn't have anything better to do, I counted the snowflakes settling on the twigs and needles of my branch. Their number was exactly 3,741,952. When the next snowflake dropped onto the branch—nothing more than nothing, as you say—the*

> *branch broke off." Having said that, the sparrow flew away.*
> *The dove thought about the story for a while and finally said*
> *to herself, "Perhaps there is only one voice lacking for peace*
> *to come in our world."*

Our one voice calling for peace or any responsible action may be nothing, but many voices with that last one added may finally make a difference. Whenever we think that our taking responsible action—be it standing up for what we believe in, working for peace and justice, or contributing time and money to good causes—may appear small in comparison to those of others, remember that when one is added to another, and then to another, great things can happen from "nothing more than nothing." In the words of Margaret Mead, "Never doubt that a small group of thoughtful, committed citizens can change the world; indeed, it's the only thing that ever has."

We have an individual and collective responsibility to serve the greater good. Collectively and collaboratively, we can choose to take responsible action in our family and working lives, and in broader social and environmental arenas.

SOCIAL AND ENVIRONMENTAL RESPONSIBILITIES

In the next chapter, we will look deeper into the role of the conscious leader, leading within a conscious business, but regardless of our leadership role, taking responsible action requires an increasing sensitivity to our social and environmental responsibilities. This requires us to take an active role in creating a better world. Theodore Roosevelt, former president of the United States, in his "Citizenship in a Republic" speech given at the Sorbonne in Paris, France, on April 23, 1910, said:

> *It is not the critic who counts; not the man who points out*
> *how the strong man stumbles, or where the doer of deeds could*
> *have done them better. The credit belongs to the man who*
> *is actually in the arena, whose face is marred by dust and*
> *sweat and blood; who strives valiantly; who errs, who comes*
> *up short again and again, because there is no effort without*

error and shortcoming; but who does actually strive to do the deeds; who knows great enthusiasms, the great devotions; who spends himself in a worthy cause; who at the best knows in the end the triumph of high achievement, and who at the worst, if he fails, at least fails while daring greatly, so that his place shall never be with those cold and timid souls who neither know victory nor defeat.[137]

There are many worthy causes to which we can dedicate our time. John Renesch reminds us in *The Great Growing Up* about taking responsibility for humanity's future by becoming a more conscious society.[138] Conscious leaders make up a conscious society and can have a significant impact on the future of humanity. Exemplifying conscious leadership, Yvon Chouinard, founder of Patagonia, says, "For us at Patagonia, a love of wild and beautiful places demands participation in the fight to save them, and to help reverse the steep decline in the overall environmental health of our planet. We donate our time, services and at least one percent of our sales to hundreds of grassroots environmental groups all over the world who work to help reverse the tide. We know that our business activity—from lighting stores to dyeing shirts—creates pollution as a by-product. So, we work steadily to reduce those harms."[139]

Because of this inspirational and conscious leadership philosophy, I have decided that proceeds from this book will be donated to social impact agencies and environmental causes.

AVOIDING THE BLAME GAME

Taking responsible action also means avoiding the blame game. Conscious leaders do not get caught up with blaming others; they take responsibility for their own actions and don't make others wrong. Political statements have been mostly avoided in this book, but I resonate with the words of John F. Kennedy who said, "Let us not seek the Republican answer or the Democratic answer, but the right answer. Let us not seek to fix the blame for the past. Let us accept our own responsibility for the future."[140] Conscious leaders don't play the blame game, and they take responsibility for the future.

Our work is often complicated, and mistakes are inevitable. One of my coaching clients shared a work situation that was becoming intolerable. When her colleague noticed a minor mistake in a report or spreadsheet, she would send my client an email alerting her to the mistake. She would also copy the vice president responsible for their department, apparently to point the finger of blame at my client. My client's discomfort with a difficult work situation was impeding any direct confrontation, but this blame game was creating a toxic work environment. In a culture where mistakes are punished, we quickly learn that mistakes are best made by someone else. People may think that pointing the blame at someone else will in some way hide their own mistakes. As Michael Carroll, author of *Awake at Work*, observed, when we fear mistakes rather than learn from them, the game of hide and blame becomes a high art.[141] Fortunately, the vice president in this case, seeing through this game and frustrated by the unnecessary emails he was receiving, requested he not be copied on emails of such insignificance but still missed the opportunity to create a "no blame" culture where mistakes are treated as learning opportunities and the practice of blaming others is not tolerated.

Finding someone to blame has become a social habit in the US, an increasingly litigious country. We have become conditioned to the blame game, assuming there's always someone to pay for any pain or injustice we may feel, and lawyers stand at the ready to sue for compensation. In business, insurance companies prefer to settle out of court and increase insurance premiums, negatively affecting business viability and increasing costs for the consumer. The blame game, whether between family members, friends, colleagues, or anyone else, saps our energy. Conscious leaders don't play the blame game.

LEADING WITH ENERGY

Taking responsible action is not always easy. Conscious leaders are proactive, resilient, high-energy leaders able to take personal responsibility for their actions; they influence the collective responsibility of those with whom they collaborate. Linda Hoopes, president of Resilience Alliance in Atlanta and a former colleague at Conner Partners, describes resilience as the ability to deal with high levels of challenge while maintaining or regaining high levels of effectiveness and well-being. Her most recent book, *Prosilience: Building Your Resilience for a Turbulent World*, provides exercises for consciously, intentionally, and proactively strengthening resilience.[142] Many of what Hoopes calls "resilience muscles" can be developed using the conscious leadership practices described in this book. I resonate with her idea that physical, mental, emotional, and spiritual energy building requires us to push beyond normal limits and then take time to recover. Leading consciously is not easy; it requires practice. Conscious leadership requires us to go beyond our self-imposed limitations and then, using the practices of noticing, setting intention, and acting responsibly, learn from the experience and replenish the energy in order to continue the journey to becoming a conscious leader.

ACTING RESPONSIBLY—TAKING RESPONSIBLE ACTION

Conscious Leadership Behaviors:

- Acting with a profound sense of responsibility for the lives entrusted to us
- Taking personal responsibility for all aspects of our lives
- Inspiring collective responsibility
- Being socially and environmentally responsible
- Serving the greater good
- Making conscious choices aligned with purpose, intentions, and commitments
- Daring greatly, knowing both success and failure, both victory and defeat
- Avoiding the blame game
- Building resilience muscles
- Leading with energy

PART IV

Organizational Leadership

CHAPTER 10

Conscious Business

The purpose of writing this book was to offer practices for aspiring conscious leaders along with practical behaviors for each of the practices. These practices for leading consciously are for leaders everywhere in all organizations and all walks of life. During my career, I have worked as a leader in various international organizations and, in my coaching and consulting role, have served as an advisor to leaders in a broad spectrum of businesses around the world. With this organizational experience and my focus on the role of conscious leaders in business, I could not complete this book without some discourse on the current and future state of conscious leadership in organizations.

Selecting the term *conscious business* as the title and theme for this chapter was a conscious choice because it embraces more than just conscious capitalism or corporate social responsibility. After reviewing the influence of Milton Friedman on capitalist thinking and the current conscious capitalism movement, I will explore six principles of conscious business in the areas of conscious leadership, stakeholder integration, conscious cultures, ethical imperatives, sustainability, and whole systems thinking. Measurement beyond the balanced scorecard and the value of leadership circles within the context of conscious business are also included.

MILTON FRIEDMAN'S INFLUENCE

Many hold the perspective that the primary purpose of business is to maximize profits or maximize shareholder value. Economist Milton Friedman declared in a 1970 *New York Times* magazine article, "There is one and only one social responsibility of business—to use its resources and engage in activities designed to increase its profits so long as it stays within the rules of the game."[143] This focus on maximizing profits is increasingly evident today in the number of activist investors becoming major shareholders and then demanding increased profitability with little regard for the people in the organization, the products and services offered, the customers and suppliers within the supply chain, or the environment in which the organization operates.

Stakeholder theory provides a contrasting perspective to Milton Friedman's shareholder focus. In 1980, Edward Freeman and Ram Charan, researchers at the University of Pennsylvania's Wharton School, wrote, "Coalitions must be built with other key stakeholder groups such as labor, consumers, and environmentalists … The organizational structure for such proactive stakeholder management must be put in place."[144] Freeman went on to publish his landmark book, *Strategic Management: A Stakeholder Approach*, in which he described a stakeholder as "any group or individual who can be or is affected by the achievement of the firm's objectives."[145] More recently, in *Firms of Endearment*, Conscious Capitalism cofounder Raj Sisodia and his fellow researchers suggested that the shareholder versus stakeholder debate presents a false dichotomy. They believe that the best way to create value for shareholders in the long run is by consciously creating value for all stakeholders. Sisodia et al. offer a list of companies they call "firms of endearment" because they strive through their words and deeds to endear themselves to all their primary stakeholders, bringing the interests of all stakeholder groups into strategic alignment, where no stakeholder group benefits at the expense of any other, and each prospers as the others do.[146] *Firms of Endearment* is on my recommended reading list, and I'm inspired by the business philosophies espoused and the companies described. However, the actions of activist investors hitting the business news pages almost daily is disturbing. Their actions, focused solely on financial performance, dampen my optimism that the growing number of customers, employees, suppliers, and other stakeholders striving for a more conscious business philosophy can withhold the onslaught of the activist investor. The need to stand up for the ideals and philosophies of conscious business is greater than ever.

CONSCIOUS CAPITALISM

Conscious capitalism is perhaps the best-known social descriptor of capitalism in use today. Other similar forms of capitalism have been described as inclusive capitalism, responsible capitalism, natural capitalism, moral capitalism, progressive capitalism, and breakthrough capitalism, to name but a few. The conscious capitalism movement was inspired by John Mackey, cofounder of Whole Foods Market, and Raj Sisodia, professor and research scholar at Babson College, with their book *Conscious Capitalism*, which describes the four pillars of conscious capitalism as higher purpose, stakeholder integration, conscious leadership, and conscious culture.[147] The conscious capitalist credo presented in the book and on the conscious capitalism website is worth including here:

> We believe that business is good because it creates value, it is ethical because it is based on voluntary exchange, it is noble because it can elevate our existence, and it is heroic because it lifts people out of poverty and creates prosperity. Free enterprise capitalism is the most powerful system for social cooperation and human progress ever conceived. It is one of the most compelling ideas we humans have ever had. But we can aspire to even more.

> Conscious Capitalism is a way of thinking about capitalism and business that better reflects where we are in the human journey, the state of our world today, and the innate potential of business to make a positive impact on the world. Conscious businesses are galvanized by higher purposes that serve, align, and integrate the interests of all their major stakeholders. Their higher state of consciousness makes visible to them the interdependencies that exist across all stakeholders, allowing them to discover and harvest synergies from situations that otherwise seem replete with trade-offs. They have conscious leaders who are driven by service to the company's purpose, all the people the business touches, and the planet we all share together.

Conscious businesses have trusting, authentic, innovative, and caring cultures that make working there a source of both personal growth and professional fulfillment. They endeavor to create financial, intellectual, social, cultural, emotional, spiritual, physical, and ecological wealth for all their stakeholders.

Conscious businesses will help evolve our world so that billions of people can flourish, leading lives infused with passion, purpose, love, and creativity; a world of freedom, harmony, prosperity, and compassion.

The conscious capitalism movement, with two major conferences each year and regional chapters in different countries, has provided a community of like-minded followers. Business leaders who have joined the movement and helped push the philosophy forward include The Container Store's Kip Tindell, Stagen Academy's Rand Stagen, Panera Bread's Ron Shaich, Starbuck's Howard Behar, Costco's James Sinegal, and Jamba Juice's James White. More heroes of Conscious Capitalism can be found on the Conscious Capitalism website.[148] Despite this broad support, future growth of this movement may be influenced by the impact of the recent acquisition of John Mackey's Whole Foods by Jeff Bezos's Amazon among other factors. The concepts of conscious capitalism appeal to people across a relatively narrow range on the political spectrum, with many on the left dismissing any form of capitalism out of hand and many on the right reluctant to accept anything other than greater shareholder value.

Inclusive capitalism is the brainchild of Lady Lynn Forester de Rothschild, chief executive officer, E.L. Rothschild, the exclusive London investment company with investments in media, asset management, energy, consumer goods, telecommunications, agriculture, and real estate worldwide. Like conscious capitalism, inclusive capitalism is not just another name for corporate social responsibility, philanthropy, or redistribution. Lady Rothschild suggests that "failings in Western capitalism are at the root of the social and political dysfunction gripping the world. Income and wealth have indeed been monopolized by the richest few, leading to widening economic inequality, stagnating wages, and a shrinking middle class. The values and priorities of our capitalist system need to evolve, as they have done many times before."[149] According to Mark Carney, governor of the Bank of England, "Inclusive Capitalism is fundamentally about delivering a basic social contract comprised of relative equality of outcomes, equality of opportunity, and fairness across generations."[150] The Coalition of Inclusive Capitalism is contributing to the debate about how to improve capitalism so that it creates long-term value that sustains human endeavor in the interest of all stakeholders.

Advocates of conscious, inclusive, and other progressive forms of free-enterprise capitalism are keen to emphasize that these movements are not about corporate social responsibility. Definitions of corporate social responsibility vary widely, but at its core, organizations espousing corporate social responsibility promote the integration of social and environmental issues in their business operations. Although many corporate social responsibility initiatives are perceived more as public relations stunts than a true integration of social and environmental concerns, many organizations are making important contributions to their communities and the world at large. Conscious leaders have a much larger vision for their conscious organizations.

Although I have been an ambassador for the conscious capitalism movement and support the philosophy of inclusive capitalism, I know the importance of language and believe that *conscious business* is a term more acceptable to people across the economic and political spectrums and can apply to organizations in the for-profit and not-for-profit world.

CONSCIOUS BUSINESS

Charitable giving and employee volunteerism, corporate social responsibility and benefit corporations, social impact agencies and other social ventures, green enterprises and sustainable businesses, are all ideas that add to the confusion surrounding conscious business. These ideas are often found inside conscious businesses but do not tell the whole story. Much of what has been written about conscious business emanates from philosopher Ken Wilber's integral model. The five fundamental parameters of the integral model are quadrants, levels, lines, states, and types. Listening to Ken Wilber describe the integral map of these parameters during my recent participation in the conscious business change agent certification program was as overwhelming as it was inspiring. As complex as this integral map sounds, Wilber, in the foreword to Fred Kofman's book *Conscious Business*, suggests that "it actually shakes down into a handful of fairly simple factors that can be quickly mastered. The easiest way to summarize the integral map is that it covers the spectrum of consciousness operating in both inner and outer worlds: the integral approach includes body, mind, and spirit in self, culture, and nature."[151]

Ken Wilber is one of the faculty of the Conscious Business Initiative program presented by Humanity's Team along with other leaders in the conscious business movement referenced in this book. This global conscious business movement of leaders, change agents, and concerned citizens of the world is dedicated to transforming business and is guided by the principles of the Conscious Business Declaration that was initiated by Humanity's Team, the Club of Budapest, the Goi Peace Foundation, and the Fowler Center for Business. Here is the Conscious Business Declaration, which at the time of writing had nearly ten thousand signatures:

> As a global community of business leaders, we are committed to developing the awareness and skills needed to evolve consciously our organizations in alignment with these principles:
>
> 1. We Are One with humanity and all of life. Business and all institutions of the human community are integral parts of a single reality—interrelated, interconnected and interdependent.
>
> 2. In line with this reality, the purpose of Business is to increase economic prosperity while contributing to a healthy environment and improving human wellbeing.
>
> 3. Business must go beyond sustainability and the philosophy of "do no harm" to restoring the self-renewing integrity of the Earth.
>
> 4. Business must operate with economic, social and ecological transparency.

5.   Business must behave as a positive and proactive member of the local and global communities in which it operates.

6.   Business that sees, honors, and celebrates the essential interconnected nature of all human beings and all life maximizes human potential and helps create a world that works for all.

7.   When aligned with Oneness, Business is the most powerful engine on Earth for creating prosperity and flourishing for all.[152]

As a certified conscious business change agent and signatory of this declaration, I am committed to supporting the conscious business movement. Combining the concepts of conscious business, conscious capitalism, inclusive capitalism, and other related initiatives has led me to define guiding principles for conscious leaders who aspire to build conscious businesses:

- **Conscious leadership:** purposefully applying the conscious leadership practices for the benefit of all
- **Stakeholder integration:** honoring the interrelationship, interconnectedness, and interdependence of all major stakeholders
- **Conscious cultures:** making the world a better place to live and work
- **Ethical imperatives:** choosing the right path for the greater good
- **Beyond sustainability:** contributing to the creation of a better world
- **Whole-systems thinking:** co-creating, uniting, and integrating the separate fragments into the oneness of the whole

Each of these six principles is explored in more detail below.

CONSCIOUS LEADERSHIP

Purposefully applying the conscious leadership practices for the benefit of all. Leading consciously is a prerequisite for doing business consciously. Creating a conscious business is not possible without conscious leadership. The conscious leadership practices presented in this book provide a framework—*noticing what is going on, setting intention,* and *acting responsibly*—that leaders can apply individually and collectively in their organizations. If you began reading this book by turning to this chapter, I invite you to explore the conscious leadership practices presented in previous chapters and summarized in the final chapter.

Leaders of conscious businesses clearly articulate their individual purpose and inspire others with a higher purpose for their organization. I have already described how Barry-Wehmiller, a manufacturing services organization with a focus on truly human leadership, defined its purpose as being "in business so that all our team members have meaningful and fulfilling lives. ... We measure success by the way we touch the lives of people."[153] Purpose is not about being the biggest or the best at something but is about doing something that really matters beyond the products and services offered by the organization. Neither is it about being purpose driven without attention on revenue and profit. An organization that fails to deliver acceptable financial performance will be unable to fulfill its purpose in the long run. However, a higher purpose is about something greater than the products, services, and financial performance of the business. It is about acting responsibly for the benefit of all.

Also referenced in the chapter about exploring purposefully was Yvon Chouinard,[154] founder and owner of Patagonia, a supplier of environmentally friendly clothes and equipment for silent sports, none of which require a motor and where reward comes in moments of connection between people and nature. In his book, *Let My People Go Surfing*, Yvon Chouinard explains why he was in business: "True, I wanted to give money to environmental causes. But even more, I wanted to create in Patagonia a model other businesses could look to in their own searches for environmental stewardship and sustainability, just as our pitons and ice axes were models for other equipment manufacturers." This purpose is supported by a mission statement: "Build the best product, cause no unnecessary harm, use business to inspire and implement solutions to the environmental crisis." Although pessimistic about the fate of the natural world, with a worsening environmental crisis, Yvon Chouinard aspired to use business to inspire and implement solutions to the environmental crisis, believing in the need to reach out to other companies to join the quest to save this planet. The purpose of Patagonia has grown far beyond environmentally friendly products built on a commitment to cause no unnecessary harm and sustained by successful business performance. Chouinard is an exemplar of conscious leadership in a conscious business.

STAKEHOLDER INTEGRATION

Honoring the interrelationship, interconnectedness, and interdependence of all major stakeholders. As we have already seen, stakeholder theory has provided a contrasting perspective to Milton Friedman's shareholder focus. Developing a stakeholder mindset is an essential requirement for a leader of a conscious business. The five major stakeholders found in most businesses, listed in a sequence that creates the acronym SPICE, are society, partners, investors, customers, and employees.[155] Society includes related communities, governmental connections, and the environment at a local and planetary scale. Partners include vendors, suppliers, and other collaborators. Investors include individual and institutional shareholders as well as lenders. Customers include the immediate purchasers of products and services as well as the end user or consumer of those products and services. Employees include current, past, and future employees and their families. John Mackey and Raj Sisodia also suggest an outer circle of stakeholders that may include competitors, activists, critics, labor unions, and the media, although, for your organization, these stakeholders may already be an integral part of your inner circle of stakeholders.[156]

Considering stakeholders as people first helps with the focus on the interrelationship, interconnectedness, and interdependence of our stakeholders. I resonated with the conscious capitalism position that "Stakeholders make up a company. They include all the people who impact, and are impacted by, a business. We must honor them as people first before treating them according to the role they happen to be playing. They all contribute to the creation of value, and it is therefore vital that they share fairly in the distribution of that value." Stakeholder integration becomes more human as we consider our daily interactions with people rather than with inanimate organizations. These human interactions are often based on the principle of reciprocity where people give back, or reciprocate, the kind of treatment they have received from another. If you help your stakeholders succeed, they will reciprocate. Practicing reciprocity can help build loyal relationships with people interested in shared success who may be able to help you through challenging times and raise your game when times are good.

Creating value for all without extracting value from any is an important principle of stakeholder integration. My consulting clients have included major suppliers to Walmart; having shelf space for products in Walmart stores was seen as critical to the successful execution of their business strategy. Sam Walton was customer focused and dedicated to lowering the cost of living for everyone, a philosophy that has continued for many years. To keep costs low and profits high, Walmart squeezed its suppliers to such an extent that they had to supply products at below cost to retain the business. Having facilitated many senior team conversations about their Walmart strategy, it was clear that Walmart was bent on extracting as much value from its suppliers as possible to create value for customers and shareholders. Although claiming to treat employees as partners, Walmart also had a reputation for keeping employee compensation and benefits as low as possible. Although there are signs of change, Walmart has not been a role model for stakeholder integration, preferring to focus on a few selected stakeholders but not all.

Leaders of conscious businesses are typically emotionally and spiritually mature, serving a higher purpose and multiple stakeholders, standing up for what is right, mastering ego, treating everyone with respect, and acting ethically for the good of all. Mercenary leadership has no place in a conscious business. This brings up the thorny issue of CEO compensation. Analyzing ratios comparing the realized compensation of chief executives with the average or median pay of typical workers is controversial but provides interesting insights. For the 350 largest companies in the US, the CEO-to-worker compensation ratio was 20:1 in 1965, peaked at 376:1 in 2000, and was at 276:1 in 2015, according to the left-leaning Economic Policy Institute.[157] Arguing about what is and is not included in the figures may be interesting for the economist, but the inequality illustrated by these ratios reflects a majority of organizations without a genuine interest in serving multiple stakeholders.

This is not simply about greed but also about the consequential behaviors of leaders throughout these organizations. A significant portion, maybe most, of CEO compensation is now in the form of performance bonuses and stock options, and it is the performance targets that drive the behavior of the leader and consequently employees across the organization. While working in one of the divisions of a Fortune 300 company recently, I found the CEO's multi-million-dollar revenue-based performance bonus to be not only a frequent topic of conversation among employees but also the determinant of most business decisions. The internally focused revenue target was not totally inappropriate, except when it was being achieved at the expense of other stakeholders, including customers, suppliers, and employees, all of whom began to lose their loyalty for this exceptional organization. The single-minded focus on financial performance can quickly result in the short-term disenfranchisement of major stakeholders with consequential losses from which it can be difficult to recover.

Stakeholder integration is not about winning at all costs. It is not about creating value for selected stakeholders by extracting value from other stakeholders. It is about responsive multilateral dialogue and mutual exchange. Stakeholder integration is about recognizing and honoring the interrelationship, interconnectedness, and interdependence of all major stakeholders, and creating value for all.

CONSCIOUS CULTURES

Making the world a better place to live and work. Conscious leaders create conscious cultures. We can see this in entrepreneurial organizations where the founder imposes their visions, goals, beliefs, values, and assumptions, and the culture emerges as the organization grows and employees share in the leader's philosophy. There are many definitions of culture, but for my touchstone, I go back to the definition from my first teacher of culture, professor emeritus at the MIT Sloan School of Management, Edgar Schein: "The culture of a group can be defined as a pattern of shared basic assumptions that was learned by a group as it solved its problems of external adaptation and internal integration, that has worked well enough to be considered valid and, therefore, to be taught to new members as the correct way to perceive, think, and feel in relation to those problems."[158] I was fortunate to spend a week listening to Edgar Schein talk about culture a few years ago. Since then, I have experienced many different business cultures and have been involved in many cultural transformation initiatives.

The negative cultures of toxic workplaces were described in chapter 8. These are examples of unconscious cultures. I want to focus here on conscious cultures. The qualities of a conscious culture include trust, accountability, caring, transparency, integrity, loyalty, and egalitarianism. These are also characteristics of conscious leaders described explicitly in this book, except perhaps for egalitarianism. In a conscious culture, there is no class system within the organizational hierarchy, no special privileges or perks for a select few, where salary differentials between the top of the organization and the front line are smaller compared to traditional organizations, and where there is an open-door policy throughout the organization and input from all employees is welcomed.

Living in South Florida, we are fortunate that Dan Cane, one of the cofounders of Blackboard Inc., known for its technology-leading virtual classrooms, has returned to the place where he grew up to form another company that has become one of the exemplars of conscious cultures. Modernizing Medicine is a fast-growing medical technology company at the forefront of providing intelligent, cloud-based electronic medical record system solutions that help physicians increase efficiencies in their medical practices while improving both treatment and business outcomes. A tour of their offices reveals tangible evidence of a modern company culture, including Zen meditation rooms, treadmill desks, healthy food, and an open environment that supports effective communication and innovation. However, as Dan Cane said during our meeting, creating and maintaining this conscious culture is primarily about hiring the right people and then talking about the culture all the time. Although there is a laser focus on products and services, Cane claims to spend 80 percent of his time on the culture, attending all new employee orientation sessions, talking to individuals and teams, and listening to all employees, many of whom sign up to speak to him during his Friday morning one-to-one sessions. Although Cane is clearly an inspirational, conscious leader, the employees have become the protectors of the culture.

I also met Diane Dagher, director of talent acquisition and engagement for Modernizing Medicine, who described the hiring process: "In hiring for culture, we actively search for people who bring not only a high level of skill or expertise to the position, but also a passion to achieve great things, to innovate, to adapt, and to grow. For us, the mission is to transform how healthcare information is created, consumed, and utilized to increase efficiency and improve outcomes. Every team member at Modernizing Medicine gets that. Whether you are an accountant, sales person, software developer, client specialist, attorney, or physician—in our company, you know that what you do not only makes a difference for Modernizing Medicine, it contributes to the monumental shift that is occurring in healthcare today"[159] Caring, hard work, and appreciation are the core of Modernizing Medicine's culture. As Cane said, "We haven't distilled our core values into pictures on the wall, but we talk about them all the time."

The Zappos online shoe company, acquired by Amazon in 2009, is a great example of cultural competence beyond employees. Vision and purpose were refined into a simple statement: "Zappos is about delivering happiness to the world," and despite Ruth Whippham's critical review in her book about how our pursuit of happiness is creating a nation of nervous wrecks, the Zappos brand has been built on its exceptional culture.[160, 161] Zappos formally defined a list of ten committable core values they were willing to hire and fire on, two of which stood out as a little different from the normal set of values: deliver WOW through service and create fun and a little weirdness. The focus on customer service was consciously ingrained from the start, but the broader culture emerged as the organization grew and has been captured in the Zappos Culture Book.[162] Initially, employees were invited to contribute up to five hundred words about the Zappos culture by answering several questions: What is the Zappos culture? What's different about it compared to other company cultures? What do you like about our culture? This invitation was subsequently extended to partners and customers. The book, available in print and online, is a great way to define a conscious culture and share it with all stakeholders, including potential employees. Like Modernizing Medicine, Zappos hires slowly and carefully, with interviews focused on cultural fit more than skills and capabilities. These organizations create their cultures consciously.

Many organizations measure employee engagement. According to the most recent Gallup State of the American Workplace Report,[163] only one-third of employees in the US workforce are engaged at work, loving their jobs and focused on making their workplace better every day. Sixteen percent of employees are actively disengaged, and the remaining 51 percent are not engaged—they're just there. In the world's best organizations, likely including many conscious businesses, 70 percent of employees are engaged at work. Engaged employees work in conscious cultures.

In *Return on Character*, respected leadership researcher, adviser, and author Fred Kiel describes four features that organizations which engage their workforces have in common. Two of these features relate to an organizational culture that is both caring and supportive.[164] Modernizing Medicine and Zappos are just two examples of conscious cultures that make the world a better place to live and work. Conscious cultures are people centered, extending beyond employees to all stakeholders as individuals and are reflected in the cultures of learning, trust, interconnectedness and interdependence, integrity and transparency, loyalty, respect, belonging, oneness, and caring.

ETHICAL IMPERATIVES

Choosing the right path for the greater good. The theme of ethical leadership gained a higher visibility from media reporting of the collapse of Enron, the phone hacking scandal at News of the World, rogue trading losses at UBS, and the disastrous Ponzi scheme created by Bernie Madoff, but unethical behavior is all too often found in daily workplace activities. The challenge for the conscious leader is to be aware of the ethical imperatives and, as conscious leadership author, Rebecca Watson, reminds us, to always choose the right path for the greater good.[165] Standing up for what is right is also an important aspect of the conscious leadership practice of acting with integrity described in a previous chapter.

Many organizations now have detailed codes of conduct, ethics training programs, and even ethics officers all focusing primarily on problems of misconduct and wrongdoing designed to clearly define the difference between right and wrong. Unfortunately, the greater challenges conscious leaders face are choices between right and right. Choosing between multiple right paths requires organizational leaders to apply the practices of leading consciously to complex decisions.

Much of my understanding and learning on right-versus-right decision-making has been drawn from the teachings of Joseph Badaracco, the John Shad professor of business ethics at Harvard Business School. Badaracco's *Defining Moments*[166] is an excellent treatise for understanding the powerful and irrevocable consequences for the lives of leaders who must make seemingly impossible decisions. Through three case examples, Badaracco presents an unorthodox yet pragmatic way to think about and resolve the right-versus-right choices organizational leaders face. Summarized below are a few of the learnings I took away from *Defining Moments*, but if these right-versus-right dilemmas keep you up at night, I highly recommend the book.

I can recall many situations where I've had to choose between two or more paths forward, when each alternative appears to be the right thing to do yet there is no way to choose more than one path. These dilemmas often involve the lives of real people. I referenced earlier in this chapter a situation where I was faced with the need to reduce the hours of a part-time worker. This was not only to save money for this membership organization but because there was insufficient work for the hours agreed by my predecessor. Reducing the number of hours appeared to be the right thing to do, matching the hours to the workload and carefully managing a deficit budget based on declining membership contributions. On the other hand, the worker was facing financial hardship, and reducing the hours by half could have resulted in a challenging personal situation with negative consequences. Reducing the hours and consequential costs was the right path forward in the context of budgetary limitations and in service to the majority of members of the organization. The worker served the organization well and was loved by the members, and with an eye to justice, compassion, and the worth of every individual, another right path forward was to find cost-reduction opportunities elsewhere, however difficult that might be. This relatively simple example illustrates conflicts of responsibility to challenge personal values and could have represented a defining moment in my leadership of this organization.

Badaracco's examples present stories of a young manager whose choice would affect him only as an individual, a department head whose decision would influence his entire organization, and a corporate executive whose actions could have much larger, societal ramifications. The challenges faced are not in simply summoning the courage to do the right thing but in deciding which right thing to do—not about *whether* to be ethical but *how* to be ethical.

Right-versus-right choices often arise as urgent, complicated, and sometimes painful issues of personal integrity and moral identity. Responsibilities to multiple stakeholders as described in the section on stakeholder integration may conflict with a leader's personal and organizational obligations. When I was first introduced to the Johnson & Johnson credo, still used today and originally crafted in 1943 by Robert Wood Johnson, a member of the company's founding family and company chairman from 1932 to 1963, I was impressed by the responsibilities and core values listed and prioritized. In general, mission statements and credos are too vague to provide much guidance for complicated right-versus-right decision-making, but the Johnson & Johnson credo has provided guiding principles for ethical decision-making and stakeholder prioritization for many years and clearly influenced the decision to pull all containers of Tylenol capsules, valued at $100 million, from the nation's shelves after six people died from taking poisoned Tylenol capsules. This was a defining moment for Johnson & Johnson and the then chairman, James Burke. It revealed, tested, and renewed the company's commitment to its ethical values described in the credo. Yet, as Badaracco illustrated, other decisions at Johnson & Johnson, such as the delay in recalling its highly successful painkiller Zomax, which was apparently implicated in at least fourteen deaths, were not so well aligned to those ethical values.

Badaracco reminds us of one of the favorite puzzles of contemporary moral philosophers: Pedro walks into a village and finds Jim holding twenty people hostage. Jim says he will kill them all unless Pedro takes a gun and kills one of the hostages. All of the hostages are innocent, so what should Pedro do? This is the ethics of consequences. It points Pedro in the direction of killing one hostage, which, if he does, will allow nineteen to live. A similar situation may be closer to home: Standing in front of a burning building, you realize that you can run to one part of the building and save a single child, or you can run to another part and save three children. In neither case is there any risk to you, but there's no way to save everyone, and you must choose between saving three children or saving one. Choosing the right path for the greater good suggests saving three children rather than one. But what if the one child was your own son or daughter? The responsibility to protect your child from danger is in conflict with saving the other three children. Guiding principles are often too general and can also be contradictory and unhelpful in choosing between right and right. These right-versus-right choices are complex, and as Oliver Wendell Holmes, one of the most distinguished US Supreme Court justices, wrote, "I do not give a fig for the simplicity on this side of complexity, but I would give my life for the simplicity on the other side of complexity."

Sleep-test ethics, described by Badaracco, suggest a person who has made the right choice can sleep soundly afterward, whereas someone who made the wrong choice cannot. We've all experienced pending decisions that keep us up at night and then, having made the decision, we sleep no better the following night. This rests on our belief that we should rely on our personal insights, feelings, and instincts when we face difficult ethical problems and can be described as the ethics of intuition. This "trust yourself" intuitive approach can be an unreliable test of right-versus-right decisions.

After exploring the revealing, testing, and shaping aspects of defining moments, Badaracco introduces four important questions to consider when faced with these right-versus-right decisions: How do my feelings and intuitions define, for me, the right-versus-right conflict? Which of the responsibilities and values in conflict have the deepest roots in my life and in communities I care about? Looking to the future, what is my way? And how can expediency and shrewdness, along with imagination and boldness, move me toward the goals I care about most strongly? The first question goes beyond the conscious leader's practice of feeling all the feelings, asking more about what your feelings tell you, aligning with the adage "we see the world not as it is but as we are." The second question about the responsibilities and values in conflict involves learning who you have been on the way to becoming who you are. This is an effort to understand which values and commitments have defined your moral identity. The third question, what is my way, is not simply about the culmination of past experiences but requires looking at critical choices as the first steps in shaping your future self, looking forward down the road, not only through the rearview mirror. The fourth question is about seeing the world as it really is and asking what will work in the world as it is, not as I want it to be.

In examining truths as a process, and the idea that "truth works," Badaracco suggests that "a defining moment for an organization is far more than a courageous executive decision or a climactic event like Johnson & Johnson's decision to recall Tylenol capsules. The final, dramatic moment is often only the final and most visible part of a complex political, psychological, and administrative process. To think otherwise is to mistake an exclamation point for the sentence that precedes it." Orchestrating a process that can make the values the leader cares about become truth in the organization is necessary to make the truth process work.

Right-versus-right choices are defining moments in which leaders with responsibilities to themselves, other people in the organization, and to society at large, reveal, test, and shape—sometimes irrevocably—their values and those of their organizations. In the modern world, lives are hectic with little time or space to contemplate these right-versus-right decisions. The practice of living mindfully and finding moments of serenity can help in determining ways to keep the immediately important from overwhelming the fundamentally important. Although mission statements and credos are often too vague to provide guidelines for right-versus-right decision-making, a clearly defined individual or organizational purpose can help guide right-versus-right decisions for the greater good of all stakeholders.

BEYOND SUSTAINABILITY

Contributing to the creation of a better world. Sustainability has become a buzzword with multiple meanings. It is time to go beyond survival to flourishing, beyond sustainability to thriveability, but let's start with clarifying how the term sustainability has been applied. Andrew Basiago, a US lawyer with advanced degrees in environmental planning, traces sustainability back to *An Essay on the Principle of Population,* written by Thomas Malthus in 1798. Malthus framed the fundamental tenet of environmentalism—namely, "that because human population tends to grow in a geometric progression while subsistence can only grow in an arithmetic progression, population growth is destined to be checked by natural resource depletion and inevitable human want and misery."[167] Basiago also reported that the theme of a sustainable world society was championed by Lester Brown, founder and president of the Worldwatch Institute, whose writings in the late 1970s and early 1980s addressed such problems as overpopulation, nonrenewable energy sources, and harm done by industrial production to the natural systems. In the early 2000s, Brown was founder and president of the Earth Policy Institute, formed to provide a vision and a road map for achieving an environmentally sustainable economy. The terms *social sustainability*, *economic sustainability*, and *environmental sustainability* have become a recognized framework for the way evaluating human choices will impact social, environmental, and business vitality. These are sometimes abbreviated in the business world as people, planet, and profit, and are known as the triple bottom line.

Social sustainability in the broadest sense refers to the alleviation of hunger and poverty, a worthwhile goal for all of humanity. In the business context, social responsibility includes a people focus relating to fair labor practices and equitable compensation, which, for the lowest paid workers, represents more than the minimum living wage; workplace safety, including health and wellness; and a range of other topics such as product responsibility, diversity, sustainable lifestyles, and the creation of conscious cultures described earlier in this chapter. Beyond the internal business operations, social sustainability may include community engagement, volunteering, and philanthropic contributions.

Environmental sustainability broadly relates to the integrity of our planetary ecosystem, where resources are not harvested faster than they can be regenerated, and waste is not released into the atmosphere faster than it can be assimilated. For businesses, environmental sustainability includes reducing consumption and waste in all aspects of business operations internally and across the extended supply chain; reducing the impact of products and services on local and global environments; and designing a future based on environmentally sustainable principles.

Economic sustainability relates to the long-term financial viability of the entity, be it a country, a company, or an individual, and implies a system of operation that satisfies current consumption without compromising future needs. The increasing levels of debt incurred by national and local governments raises economic sustainability concerns for future generations. In business, it is difficult to consider economic sustainability in isolation from social and environmental sustainability. Financial viability in a conscious business requires sustainable income and profitability while operating within the constraints of social and environmental sustainability. Conscious leaders are attentive to social, environmental, and economic sustainability at all times.

Ray Anderson's book, *Mid-Course Correction,* which describes the business transformation at Interface, Inc., provides insights into the interdependence of social, environmental, and economic sustainability.[168] In 1994, Anderson, founder of what has become the world's largest producer of modular carpet, had an epiphany that awakened him to the urgent need to set a new course toward a business focused on sustainability, using a cyclical model mimicking nature. His bold vision was to be "the first company that, by its deeds, shows the entire industrial world what sustainability is in all its dimensions: People, process, product, place and profits—by 2020—and in doing so we will become restorative through the power of influence." Its mission was to "become the first name in commercial and institutional interiors worldwide through its commitment to people, process, product, place and profits. ... We will honor the places where we do business by endeavoring to become the first name in industrial ecology, a corporation that cherishes nature and restores the environment. Interface will lead by example and validate by results, including profits, leaving the world a better place than when we began, and we will be restorative through the power of our influence in the world."[169] Mission Zero, as it became known, was focused on first attaining environmental sustainability and then becoming restorative. Anderson's philosophy of doing well by doing good was focused on three ways of working: (1) earning the goodwill of customers and their predisposition to trade and to help, avoiding greenwash, the superficial cloak of green insincerity; (2) achieving resource efficiency; and (3) by setting an example that other businesses could not ignore. Updated metrics for their carpet factories for 2016 available on the Interface Global website include energy use down by 43 percent, renewable energy use increased to 87 percent, greenhouse gas emissions down 95 percent, recycled and biobased material use up to 58 percent, water use per unit of product down 86 percent, and the environmental footprint of Interface carpet, one of the more important metrics used to track progress toward the Mission Zero goals, reduced by 35 percent since 2008. Beyond sustainability, the company is moving from a philosophy of taking nothing from the earth to becoming restorative, which Anderson described as putting back more than we take and doing good to the earth, not just doing no harm. Aligned to a higher purpose, Anderson said he came to work to help save the earth.

The Interface story is inspiring, and many organizational leaders will resonate with much of its philosophy, having applied similar thinking in their own organizations, but Chris Laszlo, Judy Sorum Brown Laszlo, and fellow researchers at Case Western Reserve University's Wetherhead School of Management suggest that to get to prosperity and flourish, we will need to go beyond our language and thinking with a new spirit "able to provide a critical boost of energy, creativity and staying power aimed at the flourishing of the individual, the organization, and the world."[170] Flourishing individuals are full of vitality, deeply in touch with their own purpose, and feel connected to others, to community, and to all life on earth. Flourishing organizations generate sustainable value for all stakeholders and, by creating value for society and nature, find ways to create even more value for their customers and investors. A flourishing world represents societies that are economically, socially, culturally, and politically thriving as well as resilient.

Whether your primary purpose relates to social, environmental, or economic sustainability, it is time to go beyond sustainability to thriving, flourishing, and increasing our contribution to the creation of a better world. Ask yourself, "What can I do to help the earth?" "What can I do to help create a better world for our children and grandchildren?" Taking care of each other, our organizations, and our planet is at the pinnacle of conscious leadership behavior.

WHOLE-SYSTEMS THINKING

Co-creating, uniting, integrating the separate fragments into the oneness of the whole. The concepts of systems thinking have been with us for decades and were made popular in organizational learning by Peter Senge as the fifth discipline, with tools and techniques aimed at destroying the illusion that the world is created of separate unrelated forces.[171] Systems thinking is an important step on the journey from dividedness to wholeness, from separateness to oneness. Dividedness is a personal pathology where examples of living a divided life, according to the founder of the Center for Courage & Renewal, Parker Palmer, include refusing to invest ourselves in our work, diminishing its quality and distancing ourselves from those it is meant to serve; making our living at jobs that violate our basic values, even when survival does not absolutely demand it; remaining in settings or relationships that steadily kill off our spirits; or harboring secrets to achieve personal gain at the expense of other people.[172] We pay a steep price for this dividedness, feeling fraudulent, anxious about being found out, and depressed at the thought of denying our own integrity. Erich Fromm, the German-born American psychoanalyst and social philosopher, sees separateness as being cutoff, helpless, and without any capacity to use our human powers; separateness is the source of intense anxiety.[173] Dividedness and separateness do not support whole-systems thinking.

Conscious leaders are natural systems thinkers with well-developed systems intelligence to complement high emotional intelligence and spiritual intelligence. They see the big picture and how the separate components of the system can be integrated into the oneness of the whole.[5] Stakeholder integration is an important application of whole-systems thinking, where all stakeholders exist in relationship with the business and each other. The organization is a system operating within a system of stakeholders inside and outside of the organization. Considering society as a stakeholder that includes the environment at a local and planetary scale allows us to embrace the entire ecosystem in our thinking about wholeness and oneness.

BEYOND THE BALANCED SCORECARD

Tools such as the balanced strategy and the balanced scorecard have long provided the basis for measuring strategy execution and operational performance in organizations. To embrace whole-systems thinking, we must go beyond balanced scorecards to include sustainability metrics for all major stakeholders. Strategy maps representing a balanced strategy with measures and targets and a balanced scorecard to measure performance have developed from the work of Robert Kaplan and David Norton, authors of seminal *Harvard Business Review* articles and the first *Balanced Scorecard* book.[174] These strategy maps began with four levels, building from the bottom up. The first level was focused on learning and growth, the people and culture dimension. The second level was focused on internal business operations, the process and technology dimension. The third level was focused externally, the customer and supplier dimension. The fourth level was focused on business performance, the financial dimension. Each lower level provided a foundation on which to build up to the higher levels.

The phrase "triple bottom line" was first coined by John Elkington, a longtime proponent of corporate social and environmental responsibility.[175] Elkington argued that companies should prepare three distinct profit and loss accounts, adding people (a socially responsible dimension), and planet (the environmental dimension), to the traditional profit dimension—the three Ps of profit, people, and planet. I would add *purpose* at the beginning of the list. Some organizations have integrated the people and planet dimensions into the more traditional balanced scorecard models to set aspirational goals.

In 2015, member countries of the United Nations adopted a set of seventeen Sustainable Development Goals (SDGs) to end poverty, protect the planet, and ensure prosperity for all as part of the 2030 Agenda for Sustainable Development.[176] Although it is unfortunate that the seventeen goals were never reduced to the vital few, each goal does have specific targets to be achieved over the fifteen years. The SDGs, also known as Global Goals, build on the perceived success of the Millennium Development Goals (MDGs). These sustainability goals, along with the 2016 Paris Agreement on climate change, provide aspirational targets for governments around the world. The degree to which progress is achieved will depend on (1) the willingness of governments to invest financially in programs that will deliver results; and (2) to what extent businesses support these ideals.

Sustainability reporting was pioneered by the Global Reporting Initiative, GRI, an independent international organization, founded in 1997.[177] More recently, the International Integrated Reporting Committee (IIRC), a global coalition of regulators, investors, companies, standard setters, the accounting profession, and NGOs, has established a vision to align capital allocation and corporate behavior to wider goals of financial stability and sustainable development through the cycle of integrated reporting and thinking.[178] Leaders in conscious businesses would do well to familiarize themselves with these reporting frameworks, selecting specific goals and measures relevant to their organizations. Extending the traditional balanced scorecard to embrace relevant goals and measures of sustainability and beyond will be a challenge to be embraced by aspiring conscious leaders.

LEADERSHIP CIRCLES

Conscious leadership in organizations can be enhanced by the application of practices and behaviors described in this book, but as we have already seen, leading consciously is not easy. Pioneering in the field of conscious leadership can be challenging and sometimes lonely. Do you ever wonder, *Who can I turn to?* You may be thinking, *There are times I feel like there's no place I can be vulnerable and uncertain because everyone has their own agenda. If only it was safe to share challenges and uncertainties with trusted people who know what it is like to be in my shoes.* As a highly successful senior executive, do you ever wonder, *Is this all there is? I'm at the top of my game, feeling confident and content with my ability to lead and with the success of my organization. But I have this feeling that there's more to do or to be. It is a persistent nagging that there's a bigger difference to be made and I could use help so I can have greater positive impact in the world.* Are you ever wide awake at 3:00 a.m., wondering, *What's all this conscious leadership about? I have achieved much more than I envisioned when I was younger, but what's next, for me and my organization? I would like a renewed sense of purpose and meaning that will take me/us to new heights but don't have anyone to talk to who will hear my wonderment with equanimity and help me sort it out.* As a consultant and coach, I have worked with many leaders who have expressed these concerns.

We can all acknowledge the value of our business networks, but as we can see from our social media contacts, some are more valuable than others. Networking is not enough for the conscious leader. As Zappos CEO Tony Hsieh recommends, stop trying to network in the traditional business sense and just try to build up the number and depth of your relationships.[179] Leadership circles provide the opportunity to develop deep and trusting relationships with peers from other organizations. The idea of wisdom circles is not new. My deepest experience of wisdom circles was on my inventure in East Africa guided by Richard Leider where, sitting around the campfire, we shared our stories and the wisdom within those stories emerged. This lightly facilitated sharing of life stories provides a way to get back in touch with the deepest part of who we are without being advised or told what to do. Executive peer group roundtables are an extension of these wisdom circles and provide not only a place for sharing our stories and being vulnerable but also a laboratory for the practices of leading consciously. Hosting these roundtables, creating the space for deep meaningful conversations and learning from each other, is one of my most fulfilling experiences as a conscious leadership coach.

In the next and final chapter of this book, we will return to the practices for leading consciously, which includes combining all the practices and using all the practices all the time.

SUMMARY OF CONSCIOUS BUSINESS PRINCIPLES

- **Conscious leadership:** purposefully applying the conscious leadership practices for the benefit of all
- **Stakeholder integration:** honoring the interrelationship, interconnectedness, and interdependence of all major stakeholders
- **Conscious cultures:** making the world a better place to live and work
- **Ethical imperatives:** choosing the right path for the greater good
- **Beyond sustainability:** contributing to the creation of a better world
- **Whole-systems thinking:** co-creating, uniting, and integrating the separate fragments into the oneness of the whole

PART V

Combining All the Practices

Noticing What Is Going On
Listening with All the Senses
Learning Relentlessly
Living Mindfully
Setting Intention
Exploring Purposefully
Thinking Possibility
Committing to Action
Acting Responsibly
Speaking Candidly
Acting with Integrity
Taking Responsible Action
Combining all the Practices
All the Practices All the Time

CHAPTER 11

All the Practices All the Time

The practices for leading consciously that provide the framework for this book and the many specific behaviors aligned to these practices can independently guide the aspiring conscious leader. The greater benefit comes from combining the practices holistically. The tenth practice is, then, *all the practices all the time*. Presented in this final chapter is a summary of all the practices and a list of who conscious leaders are and what conscious leaders do, the being and doing, harvested from the many sources referenced in this book and from my own personal leadership experience.

LISTENING WITH ALL THE SENSES

Waking up; listening generously using all the senses; feeling all the feelings; being alert to changes in ourselves, in people, and in our environment; creating the space for mindfulness; recognizing the need to stop what we are doing to be mindfully aware of our surroundings without judgment

LEARNING RELENTLESSLY

Being curious about ourselves, others, and our environment; remaining open to new ideas and insights; learning from experience; checking understanding rather than making assumptions; creating space for learning both individually and in groups; accepting mistakes and failures as learning opportunities; giving and receiving timely and constructive feedback; constantly growing in self-awareness

LIVING MINDFULLY

Being in the moment; being as well as doing; being aware of who we are and how we show up in the world, our character and presence; leading from the inside out; avoiding the drama triangle; practicing mindfulness and living mindfully every day; seeing more, hearing more, and feeling more; including more and excluding less

EXPLORING PURPOSEFULLY

Starting with why; discovering and knowing our individual life purpose and the purpose of our organization; passionately exploring opportunities always aligned to purpose; aligning vocation with avocation; leading purposefully; putting people first

THINKING POSSIBILITY

Living in a place of possibility aligned with purpose and passion; believing in sufficiency, not scarcity; living in a world of multiple right answers; celebrating what is right with the world, not what is wrong; embracing a belief in unlimited possibilities; setting intention not constrained by limiting beliefs

COMMITTING TO ACTION

Articulating a compelling vision of the future aligned to purpose and passion; making a strong personal commitment to responsible action; translating vision into clearly stated intentions that build understanding, alignment, and commitment in others; recognizing that a personal purpose-driven vision and a personal commitment to action are prerequisites for the development and implementation of an organizational vision

SPEAKING CANDIDLY

Being straightforward and unequivocal; speaking truth quietly; allowing others to express themselves with candor; delivering messages with respect and kindness; inspiring conversations that matter

ACTING WITH INTEGRITY

Going beyond doing what we say we will do, backing up words with actions, practicing what we believe is right; being honest; maintaining confidentiality; aligning actions with values, purpose, intentions, and commitments; treating everyone with respect; knowing who we are and how we show up; acting ethically for the good of all; appreciating the contributions of others; taking a stand, standing up for what is right; mastering ego; leading from the inside out with authenticity, transparency, vulnerability, humility, and stewardship

TAKING RESPONSIBLE ACTION

Choosing consciously; acting responsibly always; being socially and environmentally responsible; taking full responsibility for all aspects of our lives, and actively supporting others aspiring to take responsible action; taking personal responsibility for our impact on the world; supporting collective responsibility; leading with energy and inspiration; making a difference; serving others and the greater good

ALL THE PRACTICES ALL THE TIME

Combining all the practices, living all the practices all the time; leading consciously

BEING—CONSCIOUS LEADERS ARE:

- A force for positive change in the world
- Authentic
- Awake
- Caring
- Collaborative
- Comfortable with silence and stillness
- Compassionate
- Congruent: centered and aligned to purpose both internally and externally
- Curious
- Emotionally intelligent
- Flexible
- Fundamentally selfless
- Generous
- Good stewards of their own lives, the lives of others, and the resources of the world
- Honest, open, frank, and straightforward
- Humble
- Mindfully aware of self, others, and the environment
- Possibility thinkers
- Purposeful
- Relentless learners
- Servant leaders
- Transparent
- Vulnerable

DOING—CONSCIOUS LEADERS:

- Accept what is and who they are
- Accept their responsibilities for the well-being of others
- Act responsibly with integrity always, even when no one is looking
- Appreciate the silence
- Articulate a compelling vision of the future aligned to purpose and passion

- Balance being and relating with doing
- Bring contagious energy to every situation
- Celebrate what is right with the world rather than wallowing in what is wrong
- Create space for mindfulness
- Cultivate deep self-awareness
- Don't play the blame game
- Dream big
- Engage others in conversations that matter
- Genuinely care for people and the environment
- Guide others to greatness
- Inspire with love rather than motivate by fear
- Lead organizations with a strong sense of purpose closely related to serving people
- Live their whole lives mindfully
- Listen generously with all the senses
- Live life above the line
- Live purposefully
- Manage their emotional responses
- Open up the hearts of others
- Operate from a state of beingness
- Practice mindfulness with intention and responsible action
- Speak candidly
- Speak only to improve on the silence
- Stand up against the workplace bully
- Stand up for what is right, for what they believe in
- Strive to be the best *for* the world rather than the best *in* the world
- Take personal responsibility for their actions and their impact on the world
- Take time to create the space for meditation, reflection, and contemplation
- Treat adversity as opportunities for learning

MISTAKES LEADERS MAKE

In this book, I have focused mostly on the positive behaviors of conscious leaders. Rather than focusing on the practices and behaviors of unconscious leaders (an all-too-negative perspective for aspiring conscious leaders), a reflection on some of the mistakes leaders make on the journey to becoming conscious leaders is worth some attention. Leadership mistakes have been explored in numerous books, and it is not my intention to add a comprehensive analysis of these mistakes here. However, knowing that doing more of what doesn't work doesn't work, and in the spirit of learning relentlessly, some mistakes are worth noting on the inner journey to conscious leadership.

Joseph Jaworski, founder of the American Leadership Forum, describes a series of propositions that illustrate leadership mistakes and align well with the philosophy behind the need for this book. He suggests that the trouble with leaders in the US is: (1) their lack of self-knowledge; (2) their lack of appreciation for the nature of leadership itself; (3) their focus on concepts that separate rather than concepts that express our interconnectedness; (4) their ignorance of the world and of US interdependence, their lack of world mindedness; (5) their inattention to values, forgetting to ask, "Why?" and "What for?"; (6) their inability to make changes, to create a team to make something different happen; (7) their insufficient appreciation of the relevance of stakeholders, the implications of pluralism, and the fact that nobody is in charge, and therefore each leader is partly in charge of the situation as a whole; (8) their insufficient awareness of the context, or the external environment, of whatever it is they are responsible for doing.[180]

The idea that nobody is totally in charge and that we are all at least partially responsible is illustrated by Ben Zander's recognition that the conductor of the orchestra, although a magical figure for the audience and enjoying a leadership mystique of significant magnitude, never makes a sound.[181] Shifting his concern about whether his interpretation of the music was being appreciated by the audience and by the critics to being attentive to how effective he was at enabling the musicians to play each phrase as beautifully as they were capable. In doing this, he found leaders everywhere and musicians within the orchestra capable of leading from any chair. Leaders often make the mistake of thinking they are the only ones who can lead; they miss the opportunity for leaders to emerge when given the space to lead.

Giving others the space to lead requires a shift from focusing on self to focusing on others. A mistake some leaders make is that, in the words of Fred Kiel, "Instead of working to build a better, more sustainable model for business, for social structures, for economics, for living on a thriving and healthy planet, the decisions of self-focused leaders seem rooted in mindless, shallow self-interests that in the end benefit no one, including those leaders and the institutions they run."[182] Conscious leaders are self-aware but not self-centered.

I am often asked, "What about the people who just don't get it, who don't want to become conscious leaders?" I resonate with the sentiments of Bob Chapman and Raj Sisodia about feeding the hungry, and their answer to this question: "We don't focus on the people who don't get it. We focus on the people who do."[183] If you're reading this book, I assume you are hungry for learning about the practices for becoming a conscious leader. If you don't aspire to become a conscious leader, this book will not serve you. This is true in my coaching and consulting practice. If a leader is prepared to commit to the journey to becoming a more conscious leader, I'm willing to help. Without a high level of commitment, it would be a mistake to take on that leader as a client.

RETURN ON INVESTMENT

Although there is no guarantee that applying conscious leadership practices will make you a better leader, numerous studies have shown the benefits of awareness, mindfulness, and purposeful action for individuals and organizations. Research into leadership values, behaviors, styles, and resulting performance has demonstrated the benefits of placing attention on the way we lead. One of the most compelling research studies reflecting the practices of conscious leadership is Fred Kiel's *Return on Character*, where two of the study's most critical findings are: (1) people demonstrate character through habitual behaviors; and (2) there is an observable and consistent relationship between character-driven leaders and better business results. Raj Sisodia and his fellow researchers concluded that investors in firms of endearment—companies with humanistic cultures—stand to reap significant gains with less risk.[184] In the future, we may be able to demonstrate how conscious leadership leads to greater personal fulfillment, better business results, and major change on a worldwide scale. In the meantime, I invite you to embrace the conscious leadership practices presented in this book, and strive to make a difference for yourself, for others, and for the world around you.

THE THREE QUESTIONS

In the introduction to this book, you were encouraged to continually ask three questions:

- What are you noticing?
- What are your intentions about what you are noticing?
- What responsible actions will you take in response to what you are noticing?

Additional questions, or perhaps more specific or different ways of asking these questions relating to each series of practices, may be useful.

Noticing: What are you noticing about what is going on inside you? What are you noticing in others or in your environment? What are you noticing about your learning? What are you noticing about how you are showing up—your character and presence?

Setting intention: What is your life's purpose? What is the purpose of your organization? What is possible about the situation you are in? What are you committing to?

Acting responsibly: What is your commitment to speaking candidly? What is your commitment to acting with integrity? What responsible actions are you prepared to take in service to the greater good? What role will you take in creating a better world, a better place to live and work?

PRACTICE THE PRACTICES

The themes of *noticing what is going on, setting intention,* and *acting responsibly* provide a framework for learning about the practices for leading consciously. Using all the conscious leadership practices provides for a process of transformation on your inner journey to becoming a more conscious leader. I invite you to practice the practices and adopt the behaviors described in this book, perhaps selecting one practice each day or each week to focus on. In addition, you may wish to find an accountability partner to provide feedback and challenge you to be not so much the best *in* the world but to be the best *for* the world.

A summary of the behaviors identified for each of the practices is presented on the next few pages of this book.

CONSCIOUS LEADERSHIP BEHAVIORS—ALL THE PRACTICES, ALL THE TIME

NOTICING WHAT IS GOING ON—LISTENING WITH ALL THE SENSES

- Waking up, becoming increasingly aware of everything
- Listening attentively to others using all the senses
- Feeling all the feelings
- Developing emotional intelligence
- Being highly sensitive to emotional and physiological changes in ourselves and others
- Appreciating the silence
- Being aware of feminine and masculine values within ourselves and others
- Trusting intuitive feelings
- Managing our environment to limit distractibility; embracing distractions as messages
- Creating the space for becoming mindful of what is going on

NOTICING WHAT IS GOING ON—LEARNING RELENTLESSLY

- Being constantly curious
- Encouraging learning through curiosity
- Seeking honest feedback
- Giving effective feedback
- Accepting mistakes as learning opportunities
- Asking what can be learned from an experience
- Creating space for learning individually and in groups
- Managing polarities as interdependent elements
- Understanding negative emotional triggers and responding thoughtfully
- Using internal and external journeys to develop higher levels of consciousness

NOTICING WHAT IS GOING ON—LIVING MINDFULLY

- Practicing mindfulness every day
- Being fully present to the current situation
- Being attentive to who we are and how we show up—our character and presence
- Finding our voice, performing authentically, being the best we can be
- Living mindfully in the moment, not replaying the past or anticipating the future
- Closing the gap between simple awareness and living mindfully
- Leading from above the line
- Shifting out of the drama triangle
- Practicing the purposeful pause
- Honoring opportunities for rest and renewal

SETTING INTENTION—EXPLORING PURPOSEFULLY

- Exploring inner places in the search for purpose and meaning

- Traveling purposefully on a journey of self-discovery
- Describing an individual core purpose in ten words or less
- Having an organizational purpose focused on people
- Aligning vocation with avocation
- Leading purposefully
- Living life on purpose
- Being passionate about exploring opportunities aligned to purpose
- Setting intentions and making decisions aligned to purpose
- Making the seemingly impossible possible

SETTING INTENTION—THINKING POSSIBILITY

- Considering multiple perspectives, multiple right answers
- Doing something radically different compared to what we have done in the past
- Focusing on sufficiency rather than scarcity
- Being contagiously excited and enthusiastic about future possibilities
- Reframing negative perspectives into positive, possibility thinking
- Envisioning a meaningful future for ourselves and our organizations
- Communicating a positive and hopeful outlook for the future
- Striving to be the best *for* the world rather than the best *in* the world
- Being an edgewalker, ready to jump off the cliff and learning to fly on the way down
- Walking with the dreamers, igniting the fire of possibility

SETTING INTENTION—COMMITTING TO ACTION

- Developing a compelling expression of the desired future state
- Running purposefully toward the desired future rather than away from past experiences

- Making clear distinctions between intent (the what) and intentions (the how)
- Describing clear intentions for the journey to future possibilities
- Declaring commitment to realization of the intended outcomes of the journey
- Recognizing and taking action to address competing commitments
- Building understanding, alignment, and commitment in others
- Craving alignment of who we are with what we say and do
- Being a contribution and making a difference
- Taking personal responsibility for converting commitment into responsible action

ACTING RESPONSIBLY—SPEAKING CANDIDLY

- Speaking clearly and honestly, using language that others can understand
- Clarifying what important words mean
- Being straightforward and unequivocal with a caring mindset
- Speaking truth quietly and confidently, while always being frank and straightforward
- Delivering difficult messages with respect, courtesy, kindness, and compassion
- Fostering trust and truthfulness in all interactions
- Combining advocacy with inquiry
- Revealing in the spirit of full disclosure rather than concealing information
- Creating spaces for conversations that matter
- Saying nothing that couldn't stand as the last thing we ever say to someone

ACTING RESPONSIBLY—ACTING WITH INTEGRITY

- Doing what we say we will do, backing up our words with actions
- Being impeccable with our word

- Meeting commitments
- Treating others with dignity and respect
- Standing up for what is right
- Leading with authenticity, transparency, vulnerability, and humility
- Being a good steward for purpose, people, and the planet
- Mastering ego with awareness and understanding
- Eliminating toxicity in the workplace
- Acting with integrity even when no one is looking

ACTING RESPONSIBLY—TAKING RESPONSIBLE ACTION

- Acting with a profound sense of responsibility for the lives entrusted to us
- Taking personal responsibility for all aspects of our lives
- Inspiring collective responsibility
- Being socially and environmentally responsible
- Serving the greater good
- Making conscious choices aligned with purpose, intentions, and commitments
- Daring greatly, knowing both success and failure, both victory and defeat
- Avoiding the blame game
- Building resilience muscles
- Leading with energy

RECOMMENDED BOOKS ON CONSCIOUS LEADERSHIP

In researching this book, I reviewed many resources, including books specifically associated with conscious leadership. Many are included in the notes and references, but for those interested in reading more on the subject, and in the spirit of multiple right answers, here are a few books I found particularly inspirational.

Becoming a Conscious Leader: How to Lead Successfully in a World That's Waking Up. Gina Hayden (2016).

Conscious Business: How to Build Value through Values. Fred Kofman (2013).

Conscious Leadership and the Power of Energetic Fields. Rebecca Watson (2015).

Defining Moments: When Managers Must Choose Between Right and Right. Joseph Badaracco (1997).

Firms of Endearment: How World-Class Companies Profit from Passion and Purpose. Raj Sisodia, Jag Sheth, and David Wolfe (2014).

Liberating the Corporate Soul: Building a Visionary Organization. Richard Barrett (1998).

The 15 Commitments of Conscious Leadership: A New Paradigm for Sustainable Success. Jim Dethmer, Diana Chapman, and Kaley Warner Klemp (2014).

The Great Growing Up: Being Responsible for Humanity's Future. John Renesch (2012).

NOTES

INTRODUCTION

1   John Renesch, *The Great Growing Up: Being Responsible for Humanity's Future* (Prescott, AZ: Hohm Press, 2012).

2   Andrew Pickering, *The Mangle of Practice: Time, Agency, & Science* (Chicago: The University of Chicago Press, 1995).

3   Joseph A. Raelin, ed. *Leadership-as-Practice: Theory and Application* (New York: Routledge Studies in Leadership Research, 2016).

4   Malcolm Gladwell, *Outliers: The Story of Success* (New York: Little, Brown & Company, 2008).

5   Richard Barrett, *Liberating the Corporate Soul: Building a Visionary Organization* (Woburn, MA: Butterworth-Heinemann, 1998).

6   Paul G. Ward, "Full Spectrum Leadership Behavior: An Exploratory Case Study" (PhD diss., Capella University, Minneapolis, MN, 2006). Available from ProQuest Dissertations and Theses database (UMI No. 3208075).

7   "Future Shapers," accessed January 27, 2018, www.futureshapers.com.

CHAPTER 1

8   Thomas Merton, *Seeds*, ed. Robert Inchausti (Boston, MA: Shambala, 2002).

9   Antonio D'Amasio and Gil B. Carvalho, "The nature of feelings: Evolutionary and neurobiological origins," *Nature Reviews. Neuroscience* 14, no. 2 (2013). doi: http://dx.doi.org/10.1038/nrn3403.

10   Alan Watkins, *4D Leadership: Competitive Advantage Through Vertical Leadership Development* (London: Kogan-Page, 2016).

11   Howard Gardner, *Frames of Mind: The Theory of Multiple Intelligences* (New York: Basic Books, 1993).

12   Daniel Goleman, *Emotional Intelligence: Why It Can Matter More Than IQ* (New York: Bantam Books, 1995).

13   Daniel Goleman, *Working with Emotional Intelligence* (New York: Basic Books, 1998).

14 Daniel Goleman, Richard Boyatzis, & Annie McKee, *Primal Leadership, Realizing the Power of Emotional Intelligence* (Boston, MA: Harvard Business School Press, 2002).

15 Paul G. Ward, "Full Spectrum Leadership Behavior: An Exploratory Case Study" (PhD diss., Capella University, Minneapolis, MN, 2006). Available from ProQuest Dissertations and Theses database (UMI No. 3208075).

16 "Complete Coherence Universe of Emotions Application," accessed February 6, 2018. http://www.complete-coherence.com/universeofemotions/.

17 Matthew B. Crawford, *The World Beyond Your Head: On Becoming an Individual in an Age of Distraction* (New York: Farrar, Straus and Giroux, 2015).

18 Joseph Luft and Harry Ingham, "The Johari Window, A Graphic Model of Interpersonal Awareness," in *Proceedings of the Western Training Laboratory in Group Development* (Los Angeles: University of California, Los Angeles, 1955).

19 Joseph Luft, *Of Human Interaction* (Palo Alto, CA: Mayfield Publishing Company, 1969).

20 Shelley Reciniello, *The Conscious Leader: 9 Principles and Practices to Create a Wide-awake and Productive Workplace* (Greenwich, CT: LID Publishing, 2014).

21 Kevin Cashman, *Leadership from the Inside Out: Becoming a Leader for Life* (Oakland, CA: Berrett-Koehler, 2017).

22 Nathaniel Branden, *The Art of Living Consciously: The Power of Awareness to Transform Everyday Life* (New York: Simon & Schuster, 1997).

23 Richard Barrett, *Liberating the Corporate Soul: Building a Visionary Organization* (Woburn, MA: Butterworth-Heinemann, 1998).

24 John Gerzema, & Michael D'Antonio, *The Athena Doctrine: How Women (and Men Who Think Like Them) Will Rule the Future* (San Francisco: Jossey-Bass, 2013).

25 Nilima Bhat, & Raj Sisodia, *Shakti leadership: Embracing Masculine and Feminine Power in Business* (Oakland, CA: Berrett-Koehler, 2016).

26 "This I Believe Essays," accessed February 5, 2018, http://thisibelieve.org/.

27 Rebecca Watson, *Conscious Leadership and the Power of Energetic Fields* (Bloomington, IN: AuthorHouse, 2015).

28 Janice Marturano, *Finding the Space to Lead: A Practical Guide to Mindful Leadership* (New York: Bloomsbury Press, 2014).

29 Jon Kabat-Zinn, *Wherever You Go There You Are: Mindfulness Meditation for Everyday Life* (1994).

30 Walter Mischel and Ebbe. B. Ebbesen, "Attention in delay of gratification." *Journal of Personality and Social Psychology 16,* no. 2, (1970), 329–337. doi: http://dx.doi.org/10.1037/h0029815.

CHAPTER 2

31 Stephen R. Covey, *The Seven Habits of Highly Effective People* (New York: Simon & Schuster, 1989).

32 Craig and Patricia Neal, w. Cynthia Wold, *The Art of Convening: Authentic Engagement in Meetings, Gatherings, and Conversations* (San Francisco: Berrett-Koehler, 2011).

33 Daryl Conner, *Learning as a Foundation of Our Work* (2011). Available at http://www.connerpartners.com/daryl-conner/blog.

34 John Renesch, *The Great Growing Up: Being Responsible for Humanity's Future* (Prescott, AZ: Hohm Press, 2012).

35 F. Scott Fitzgerald, *The Crack-Up* (1936), accessed February 5, 2018, http://www.esquire.com/lifestyle/a4310/the-crack-up/.

36 *The Kybalion: The Principle of Polarity* (Yogi Publication Society, 1908).

37 Jerry B. Harvey, *The Abilene Paradox and Other Meditations on Management* (New York: Lexington Books, 1988).

38 Barry Johnson, B. *Polarity Mapping: Identifying and Managing Unsolvable Problems* (Amherst, MA: HRD Press, 1996).

39 Alan Watkins, *4D Leadership: Competitive Advantage Through Vertical Leadership Development* (London: Kogan-Page, 2016).

40 "Science and Non-Duality (SAND)," accessed February 6, 2018, https://www.scienceandnonduality.com/about/nonduality/.

41 Daniel Goleman, *Emotional Intelligence: Why It Can Matter More Than IQ* (New York: Bantam Books, 1995).

42 Stephen R. Covey, *The Seven Habits of Highly Effective People* (New York: Simon & Schuster, 1989).

43 Nilima Bhat and Raj Sisodia, *Shakti leadership: Embracing Masculine and Feminine Power in Business* (Oakland, CA: Berrett-Koehler, 2016).

44 Mariana Bozesan, "The Making of a Consciousness Leader in Business: An Integral Approach" (PhD diss., Institute of Transpersonal Psychology, Palo Alto, 2009). Available from ProQuest Dissertations and Theses database (UMI No. 3318116).

CHAPTER 3

45 Thich Nhat Hanh. *The Miracle of Mindfulness: A Manual on Meditation* (Boston: Beacon Press, 1987).

46 Abraham H. Maslow, *Toward a Psychology of Being,* 3rd ed. (New York: John Wiley, 1999).

47 Kevin Cashman, *Leadership from the Inside Out: Becoming a Leader for Life*, 3rd ed. (Oakland, CA: Berrett-Koehler, 2017).

48 Daryl Conner, "The Basics of Character/Presence" (The Conner Academy), accessed February 6, 2018, http://conneracademy.com/.

49 Fred Kiel, *Return on Character: The real reasons leaders and their companies win* (Boston, MA: Harvard Business Review Press, 2015).

50 Edward O. Wilson, *Consilience: The unity of knowledge* (Toronto, CAN: Random House, 1999).

51 Phakyab Rinpoche and Sofia Stril-Rever, *Meditation Saved my Life: A Tibetan Lama and the Healing Power of the Mind* (Novato, CA: New World Library, 2017).

52 Lance H. K. Secretan, *The Spark, the Flame, and the Torch: Inspire Self, Inspire Others, Inspire the World* (Toronto, CA: The Secretan Center, 2010).

53 Kevin Cashman, *Leadership from the Inside Out: Becoming a Leader for Life*, 3rd ed. (Oakland, CA: Berrett-Koehler, 2017).

54 Daryl Conner, "The Importance of Character and Presence," accessed February 6, 2018, http://www.connerpartners.com/daryl-conner/blog.

55 Bruce Molsky, accessed February 6, 2018, https://www.brucemolsky.com.

56 Alan Seale, *Create a World That Works: Tools for Personal and Global Transformation* (San Francisco: Red Wheel, 2011).

57 Ken Wilber, "All Quadrants All Levels," accessed February 6, 2018, https://integrallife.com/.

58 Jim Dethmer, Diana Chapman, and Kayley Warner Klemp, *The 15 Commitments of Conscious Leadership: A New Paradigm for Sustainable Success.* (2014).

59 Stephen B. Karpman, "Fairy Tales and Script Drama Analysis." Transactional Analysis Bulletin, 7, no. 26, (1968) 39–43.

60 David Emerald, *The Power of Ted: The Empowerment Dynamic* (Bainbridge Island, WA: Polaris Publishing, 2016).

61 David Emerald, *The Power of Ted: The Empowerment Dynamic.* (Bainbridge Island, WA: Polaris Publishing, 2016).

62 Nilima Bhat and Raj Sisodia, *Shakti leadership: Embracing Masculine and Feminine Power in Business* (Oakland, CA: Berrett-Koehler, 2016).

63 "The Conscious Leadership Group," accessed December 3, 2017, http://conscious.is/resources.

64 Erich Fromm, *The Art of Loving* (New York: Harper & Row, 1956).

65 Michael Carroll, *The Mindful Leader: Awakening Your Natural Management Skills Through Mindfulness Meditation* (Boston, MA: Trumpeter Books, 2007).

66 Chris Laszlo and Judy Sorum Brown, *Flourishing Enterprise: The New Spirit of Business* (Stanford, CA: Stanford University Press, 2014).

67   David Whyte, *River Flow: New and Selected Poems 1984–2007* (Langley, WA: Many Rivers Press, 2007).

68   Marek Vich, "The Emerging Role of Mindfulness Research in the Workplace and its Challenges." *Central European Business Review,* 4 no. 3, (2015).

69   Mindful Nation UK, "Report by the Mindfulness All-Party Parliamentary Group (MAPPG)," (2015), www.themindfulnessinitiative.org.uk.

CHAPTER 4

70   Simon Sinek, *Start with Why: How Great Leaders Inspire Everyone to Take Action* (New York: Portfolio, 2009).

71   Richard Leider, *The Power of Purpose: Find Meaning, Live Longer, Better*, 3rd ed. (Oakland, CA: Berrett-Koehler, 2015).

72   Alan Seale, *Soul Mission, Life Vision: Recognize Your True Gifts and Make Your Mark in the World* (San Francisco: Red Wheel, 2003).

73   Roy M. Spence, *It's Not What You Sell, It's What You Stand For* (New York: Portfolio, 2009).

74   "The Purpose Prize," accessed December 3, 2018, http://www.aarp.org/about-aarp/purpose-prize/.

75   Viktor E. Frankl, *Man's Search for Meaning: An Introduction to Logotherapy* (Boston, MA: Beacon Pres, 1992).

76   Roy M. Spence, *It's Not What You Sell, It's What You Stand For* (New York: Portfolio, 2009).

77   Yvon Chouinard, *Let My People Go Surfing: The Education of a Reluctant Businessman* (New York: Penguin Books 2016).

78   Bob Chapman and Raj Sisodia, *Everybody Matters: The Extraordinary Power of Caring for Your People Like Family* (New York: Portfolio, 2015).

79   Herman Hesse, *Demian* (Middletown, RI: BN Publishing, 2008).

CHAPTER 5

80   Norman Vincent Peale, *The Power of Positive Thinking* (New York: Prentice-Hall, 1952).

81   Rosamund S. Zander and Ben Zander, *The Art of Possibility: Transforming Professional and Personal Life* (Boston, MA: Harvard Business School Press, 2000).

82   Brené Brown, *Daring Greatly: How the Courage to Be Vulnerable Transforms the Way We Live, Love, Parent, and Lead* (New York: Avery, 2012).

83   Dewitt Jones, "Celebrate What's Right with the World," (2017) video.

84 Rosamund S. Zander and Ben Zander, *The Art of Possibility: Transforming Professional and Personal Life* (Boston, MA: Harvard Business School Press, 2000).

85 Joseph Jaworski, *Synchronicity: The Inner Path of Leadership* (Oakland, CA: Berrett-Koehler, 2011).

86 Kevin Cashman, *Leadership from the Inside Out: Becoming a Leader for Life,* 3rd ed. (Oakland, CA: Berrett-Koehler, 2017).

87 Prentice Mulford, *Thoughts are Things* (Middletown, RI: BN Publishing, 2008).

88 Lion Goodman, *Clear Your Beliefs: Delete Your Limiting Beliefs, Transform Your Life, and Unleash Your Magnificence,* (2010), http://www.transformyourbeliefs.com/.

89 Lance H. K. Secretan, *The Spark, the Flame, and the Torch: Inspire Self, Inspire Others, Inspire the World* (Toronto, CA: The Secretan Center, 2010).

90 Judi Neal, *Edgewalkers: People and Organizations That Take Risks, Build Bridges, and Break New Ground* (Westport, CT: Praeger Publishers, 2006).

91 Mark Nepo, *Facing the Lion, Being the Lion: Finding Inner Courage Where It Lives* (San Francisco, Canari Press, 2007).

CHAPTER 6

92 The United States Marine Corps. *Warfighting: Tactics for Managing Confrontation* (New York: Doubleday, 1994).

93 Fred Kofman, *Conscious Business: How to Build Value Through Values* (Boulder, CO: Sounds True, 2013).

94 Mariana Bozesan, "The Making of a Consciousness Leader in Business: An Integral Approach" (PhD diss., Institute of Transpersonal Psychology, Palo Alto, 2009). Available from ProQuest Dissertations and Theses database (UMI No. 3318116).

95 Rosamund S. Zander, & Ben Zander, *The Art of Possibility: Transforming Professional and Personal Life* (Boston, MA: Harvard Business School Press, 2000).

96 William Bridges, *Transitions: Making Sense of Life's Changes* (New York: Addison-Wesley, 1980).

97 Daryl Conner, *Managing at the Speed of Change: How Resilient Managers Succeed and Prosper Where Others Fail* (New York: Random House, 2006).

98 "An Evening with Robert Kegan and Immunity to Change," (2012), https://www.youtube.com/watch?v=FFYnVmGu9ZI.

CHAPTER 7

99 Fred Kofman, *Conscious Business: How to Build Value through Values* (Boulder, CO: Sounds True, 2013).

100 Bob Chapman and Raj Sisodia, *Everybody Matters: The Extraordinary Power of Caring for Your People Like Family* (New York: Portfolio, 2015).

101 Subir Chowdhury, *The Difference: When Good Enough Isn't Enough* (New York: Crown Business, 2017).

102 Gary Chapman, *Love as a Way of Life: Seven Keys to Transforming Every Aspect of your Life* (Colorado Springs, CO: Waterbrook Press, 2008).

103 Jim Dethmer, Diana Chapman, and Kayley Warner Klemp, *The 15 Commitments of Conscious Leadership: A New Paradigm for Sustainable Success.* (2014).

104 Roger Walsh, *Essential Spirituality: The 7 Central Practices to Awaken Heart and Mind* (New York: John Wiley, 1999).

105 Dennis S. Reina and Michelle L. Reina, *Trust and Betrayal in the Workplace: Building Effective Relationships in Your Organization* (Oakland, CA: Berrett-Koehler, 1999).

106 Craig and Patricia Neal, w. Cynthia Wold, *The Art of Convening: Authentic Engagement in Meetings, Gatherings, and Conversations* (San Francisco: Berrett-Koehler, 2011).

107 Ben Zander, "The transformative power of classical music," (TED: 2008), https://www.ted.com/talks/benjamin_zander_on_music_and_passion.

CHAPTER 8

108 Don Miguel Ruiz, *The Four Agreements: A Practical Guide to Personal Freedom* (San Rafael, CA: Amber-Allen Publishing, 1997).

109 Lynne Twist, *The Soul of Money: Transforming Your Relationship With Money and Life* (New York: W. W. Norton & Company, 2003).

110 Gary Chapman, *Love as a Way of Life: Seven Keys to Transforming Every Aspect of your Life* (Colorado Springs, CO: Waterbrook Press, 2008).

111 Kevin Cashman, *Leadership from the Inside Out: Becoming a Leader for Life,* 3rd ed. (Oakland, CA: Berrett-Koehler, 2017).

112 Michael Carroll, *Awake at Work: Facing the Challenges of Life on the Job* (London: Shambhala, 2004).

113 Gina Hayden, *Becoming a Conscious Leader: How to Lead Successfully in a World That's Waking Up* (Bideford, UK: Panacea Books, 2016).

114 Chris Laszlo and Judy Sorum Brown, *Flourishing Enterprise: The New Spirit of Business* (Stanford, CA: Stanford University Press, 2014).

115 Mark Moreland, interview by David Reimer, & Sonja Meighan, "Executive Roundtable: Candor and Transparency in the C-Suite." People & Strategy, 39 no. 4, (2006), 42–45.

116 Bob Johansen, *Leaders Make the Future: Ten New Leadership Skills for an Uncertain World,* 2nd ed. (San Francisco, CA: Berrett-Koehler, 2012).

117 Ellen van Velsor, Cynthia D. McCauley, and Marian N. Ruderman, *The Center for Creative Leadership Handbook of Leadership Development,* 3rd ed. (San Francisco: Jossey-Bass, 2010).

118 Brené Brown, B. *Daring Greatly: How the Courage to Be Vulnerable Transforms the Way We Live, Love, Parent, and Lead* (New York: Avery, 2012).

119 Michael Carroll, *The Mindful Leader: Awakening Your Natural Management Skills Through Mindfulness Meditation* (Boston, MA: Trumpeter Books, 2007).

120 Robert K. Greenleaf, *Servant Leadership: A Journey into the Nature of Legitimate Power and Greatness* (New York: Paulist Press, 1977).

121 Jim Collins, *Good to Great: Why Some Companies Make the Leap and Others Don't* (New York: HarperCollins, 2001).

122 Edgar H. Schein, *Humble Inquiry: The Gentle Art of Asking Instead of Telling* (Oakland, CA: Berrett-Koehler, 2013).

123 Peter Block, *Stewardship: Choosing Service Over Self-Interest,* 2nd ed. (San Francisco: Berrett-Koehler, 2013).

124 Roy M. Spence, *It's Not What You Sell, It's What You Stand For* (New York: Portfolio, 2009).

125 Jim Collins, *Good to Great: Why Some Companies Make the Leap and Others Don't* (New York: HarperCollins, 2001).

126 Rosalie Chamberlain, *Conscious Leadership in the Workplace: A Guidebook to Making a Difference One Person at a Time* (New York: Morgan James, 2016).

127 Gina Hayden, *Becoming a Conscious Leader: How to Lead Successfully in a World That's Waking Up* (Bideford, UK: Panacea Books, 2016).

128 Andrew Faas, *From Bully to Bull's-Eye: Move Your Organization Out of the Line of Fire* (Toronto, CAN: RCJ Press, 2016).

129 Judith L. Fisher-Blando, "Workplace Bullying: Aggressive Behavior and its Effect on Job Satisfaction and Productivity." (Doctoral diss., University of Phoenix, 2008). Available from ProQuest Dissertations and Theses database, (UMI No. 3309257).

130 Bill Hybels, *Who You Are When No One's Looking: Choosing Consistency, Resisting Compromise* (Downers Grove, IL: InterVarsity Press, 1987).

CHAPTER 9

131 Joel Barker, "The Star Thrower Story," accessed February 6, 2018, https://starthrower.com/pages/the-star-thrower-story.

132 Gina Hayden, *Becoming a Conscious Leader: How to Lead Successfully in a World That's Waking Up* (Bideford, UK: Panacea Books, 2016).

133 Lisa Severy, Jack and Phoebe Ballard, *Turning points: Managing Career Transitions with Meaning and Purpose* (Bloomington, IN: Author House, 2008).

134 Michael Carroll, *The Mindful Leader: Awakening Your Natural Management Skills Through Mindfulness Meditation* (Boston, MA: Trumpeter Books, 2007).

135 Bob Chapman and Raj Sisodia, *Everybody Matters: The Extraordinary Power of Caring for Your People Like Family* (New York: Portfolio, 2015).

136 Joseph Jaworski, *Synchronicity: The Inner Path of Leadership* (Oakland, CA: Berrett-Koehler, 2011).

137 Theodore Roosevelt, "Citizenship in a Republic," April 23, 1910, Sorbonne University, Paris, France.

138 John Renesch, *The great growing up: Being Responsible for Humanity's Future* (Prescott, AZ: Hohm Press, 2012).

139 Yvon Chouinard, *Let My People Go Surfing: The Education of a Reluctant Businessman* (New York: Penguin Books 2016).

140 John F. Kennedy, Speech at Loyola College Alumni Banquet, Baltimore, Maryland, February 18, 1958. Papers of John F. Kennedy.

141 Michael Carroll, *Awake at Work: Facing the Challenges of Life on the Job.* (London: Shambhala, 2004).

142 Linda L. Hoopes, *Prosilience: Building your Resilience for a Turbulent World* (Decatur, GA: Dara Press, 2017).

CHAPTER 10

143 Milton Friedman, "The social responsibility of business is to increase profits," *New York Times Magazine*, September 13, 1970.

144 Ram Charan and R. Edward Freeman, "Planning for the Business Environment of the 1980s." *Journal of Business Strategy*. 1, no. 2 (Fall 1980).

145 R. Edward Freeman, *Strategic management: A Stakeholder Approach* (London, UK: Pitman Publishing, 1984).

146 Raj Sisodia, Jag Sheth, and David Wolfe, *Firms of Endearment: How World Class Companies Profit from Passion and Purpose*, 2nd ed. (Upper Saddle River: Pearson Education, 2014).

147 John Mackey and Raj Sisodia, *Conscious Capitalism: Liberating the Heroic Spirit of Business* (Boston: Harvard Business School Publishing, 2014).

148 "Heroes of Conscious Capitalism," accessed February 6, 2018, https://www.consciouscapitalism.org/heroes.

149 Lady Lynn Forester de Rothschild, "Restoring Capitalism's Good Name," (2016), http://time.com/4587730/lynn-forester-de-rothschild-inclusive-capitalism/.

150 Mark Carney, "Keynote," Coalition for Inclusive Capitalism Conference, 2014, https://www.inc-cap.com/videos/mark-carney-keynote-speech/.

151 Fred Kofman, *Conscious Business: How to Build Value through Values* (Boulder, CO: Sounds True, 2013).

152 "Conscious Business Declaration," accessed February 6, 2018, https://www.humanitysteam.org/.

153 Bob Chapman and Raj Sisodia, *Everybody Matters: The Extraordinary Power of Caring for Your People Like Family* (New York: Portfolio, 2015).

154 Yvon Chouinard, *Let My People Go Surfing: The Education of a Reluctant Businessman*, (New York: Penguin Books 2016).

155 Raj Sisodia, Jag Sheth, and David Wolfe, *Firms of Endearment: How World Class Companies Profit from Passion and Purpose*, 2nd ed. (Upper Saddle River: Pearson Education, 2014).

156 John Mackey and Raj Sisodia, *Conscious Capitalism: Liberating the Heroic Spirit of Business* (Boston: Harvard Business School Publishing, 2014).

157 Economic Policy Institute, accessed December 3, 2017, http://www.epi.org/.

158 Edgar Schein, *Organizational Culture and Leadership*, 3rd ed. (San Francisco: Jossey-Bass, 2004).

159 Diane Dagher, "Modernizing Medicine," accessed December 3, 2017, https://www.modmed.com/.

160 Tony Hsieh, *Delivering Happiness: A Path to Profits, Passion, and Purpose* (New York: Grand Central Publishing, 2009).

161 Ruth Whippman, *America the Anxious: How our Pursuit of Happiness is Creating a Nation of Nervous Wrecks* (New York: St. Martin's Press, 2016).

162 Zappos Culture Book, (2014), https://www.zapposinsights.com/culture-book.

163 "Gallup State of the American Workplace Report," accessed December 3, 2017, http://www.gallup.com/.

164 Fred Kiel, *Return on Character: The Real Reasons Leaders and Their Companies Win* (Boston, MA: Harvard Business Review Press, 2015).

165 Rebecca Watson, *Conscious Leadership and the Power of Energetic Fields* (Bloomington, IN: AuthorHouse, 2015).

166 Joseph L. Badaracco, *Defining Moments: When Managers Must Choose Between Right and Right* (Boston: Harvard Business School Press, 1997).

167 Andrew D. Basiago, "Economic, Social, and Environmental Sustainability in Development Theory and Urban Planning Practice." *Environmentalist* Jun/July 19, no. 2; (1998); 145.

168 Ray C. Anderson, *Mid-Course Correction. Toward a Sustainable Enterprise: The Interface Model* (White River Junction, VT: Chelsea Green Publishing, 1998).

169 "Interface Sustainability," accessed December 3, 2017, http://www.interfaceglobal.com/.

170 Chris Laszlo, & Judy Sorum Brown, *Flourishing Enterprise: The New Spirit of Business* (Stanford, CA: Stanford University Press, 2014).

171 Peter M. Senge, *The Fifth Discipline: The Art and Practice of the Learning Organization* (New York: Currency Doubleday, 1990).

172 Parker J. Palmer, *A Hidden Wholeness: The Journey Toward an Undivided Life* (San Francisco: Jossey-Bass, 2004).

173 Erich Fromm, *The Art of Loving* (New York: Harper & Row, 1956).

174 Robert S. Kaplan and David P. Norton, *The Balanced Scorecard: Translating Strategy into Action* (Boston, MA: Harvard Business School Press, 1996).

175 "The 2030 Agenda for Sustainable Development," accessed February 6, 2018, http://www.un.org/sustainabledevelopment/.

176 John Elkington, *Cannibals with Forks: The Triple Bottom Line of 21st Century Business* (Mankato, MN: Capstone Press, 1997).

177 The Global Reporting Initiative (GRI). Retrieved from https://www.globalreporting.org.

178 The International Integrated Reporting Committee (IIRC). Retrieved from http://integratedreporting.org/.

179 Tony Hsieh, *Delivering Happiness: A Path to Profits, Passion, and Purpose* (New York: Grand Central Publishing, 2009).

CHAPTER 11

180 Joseph Jaworski, *Synchronicity: The Inner Path of Leadership* (Oakland, CA: Berrett-Koehler, 2011).

181 Rosamund S. Zander, & Ben Zander, *The Art of Possibility: Transforming Professional and Personal Life* (Boston, MA: Harvard Business School Press, 2000).

182 Fred Kiel, *Return on Character: The Real Reasons Leaders and Their Companies Win* (Boston, MA: Harvard Business Review Press, 2015).

183 Bob Chapman and Raj Sisodia, *Everybody Matters: The Extraordinary Power of Caring for Your People Like Family* (New York: Portfolio, 2015).

184 Raj Sisodia, Jag Sheth, and David Wolfe, *Firms of Endearment: How World Class Companies Profit from Passion and Purpose,* 2nd ed. (Upper Saddle River: Pearson Education, 2014).

INDEX

entitlement 106
environmental sustainability 147
equality 101, 133
ethical imperatives 129, 135, 142, 153
exclusivity 33, 80

F

Faas, Andrew 108, 110
facing the lion 71, 72, 178
father 7, 8, 23, 27, 68, 69
fear 6, 11, 29, 38, 64, 68, 104, 107-109, 161
feedback 13, 22-25, 35, 96, 165, 166
    constructive feedback 19, 22-24, 158
    effective feedback 22, 25, 35, 166
    sandwich technique 24
    uninvited feedback 24
feminine values 12
Fisher-Blando, Judith 109
flourishing 49, 92, 135, 146, 149
Frankl, Viktor 29, 58
Freedman, Marc 57
freedom 13, 29, 91, 101, 132
Freeman, Edward 130
Friedman, Milton 129, 130, 137
Fromm, Erich 49, 150
Frost, Robert 58, 119

G

generative 66, 67, 72
generosity 63, 66, 67, 105
Goodman, Lion 69
gossip 111
grandchildren 4, 29, 149
grandfather 67
Greenleaf, Robert 105
growth 20-23, 29, 151

H

Hanh, Thich Nhat 37, 175

happiness 58, 93, 141
harmless 94, 96
Hayden, Gina 103, 108
Hesse, Herman 61
higher purpose 47, 51, 131, 136, 138, 149
Hoopes, Linda 125
hot-air balloon 65
Hsieh, Tony 152
humility 12, 67, 99, 102, 104-106, 114, 115, 159, 169
Hybels, Bill 114

I

influence zone 41
inquiry 96, 98, 106, 108, 168
inspiration 57, 63, 69, 92, 117, 120, 159
inspire with love 161
integral model 133
integrity 41, 84, 89, 99-115, 121, 140-150, 159-160, 164, 168
intent 70, 76-85, 91, 96, 168
intent architect 70
interconnectedness 135-142, 153, 162
interdependence 135-142, 148, 153, 162
Interface, Inc. 148
intuition 11, 12, 20, 71, 145
inventure 33, 34, 55, 56, 71, 153

J

Jaworski, Joseph 67, 121, 162
Johansen, Bob 104
Johari Awareness Model 9
Johnson, Barry 27
Johnson & Johnson 144, 146
Jones, Dewitt 64
journeys 33, 35, 71, 166
    inner journey 31-35, 46, 55, 62, 71, 103

transformational presence 45
transparency 99, 102-104, 115, 134,
    140, 142, 159, 169
triggers 28-35, 166
triple bottom line 147, 151
true fans 43, 44
trust 12, 42, 76, 90, 93-95, 98, 103,
    140, 142, 168
turning points 33, 119

U

unequivocal 89, 92, 98, 159, 168

V

values 6, 12, 18, 39-42, 76, 99, 101,
    139-150, 159, 163, 165
values assessment 12
victimhood 47, 107, 109
vision 26, 55, 70, 71, 75, 101, 133, 141,
    148, 152, 158, 160
vocation 58, 61, 62, 158, 167
Volkswagen 114
vulnerability 12, 64, 99, 102, 104-105,
    114, 115, 159, 169

W

wakefulness 56
waking up 3, 18, 45, 157, 165
Walmart 138
Watkins, Alan 6, 27, 46
Watson, Rebecca 13, 142
White Queen 63
wholeness 39, 150
whole-systems thinking 135, 149,
    150, 153
Whyte, David 50
Wilber, Ken 45, 133, 134
wilderness journey 21, 33, 37
willingness 67, 151
Wilson, Woodrow 5
withholding 93, 94, 108

workplace bullying 99, 108, 109,
    113, 114

Z

Zander, Ben and Rosamund 63, 66,
    70, 79, 162
Zappos 141, 142, 152
Zen 3, 38, 140